What Others Are

GORDON BANKS · Former Dallas Cowboy, 8 year NFL veteran · Stanford Graduate— "Outstanding and insightful information. I learned more about communication in one workshop than my entire professional career. I highly recommend it to every professional person."

CAROL J. BOOTH · Greg Booth & Associates— "Even though, as photographers, we are trained to visually communicate, your Life Language Seminar is improving our abilities to verbally communicate. Understanding both the positive and negative characteristics of my own communication techniques, as well as those of others, has actually been a freeing experience. Thanks for the extra time and effort you have given us.

KRIS CHESKY, PhD · Professor — "The Behavioral Life Languages concept and the Kendall Life Language Profile provide a serious, analytical approach to measuring and quantifying communication types, range and intensity. It provides a means of understanding and communicating by individuals, departments, corporations and families."

AL COOPER · Founder/President Prime Time Christian Broadcasting, Inc.— "Fred and Anna have an on-going television series on our network which reaches about one million viewers. It is one of our most popular programs because it touches people where they live and helps to strengthen communication and relationships."

CLIFFORD AND PAMELA FRAZIER · Pastors and Marriage Conference Speakers · Heartline Ministries— "Don't keep the secret to yourself. Tell everybody you know that the answers they have been looking for regarding marital communication are found in *Speaking of Love*."

FRANCIS GALLOWAY • Retired Corporate Executive— "The Life Languages will greatly enhance communication wherever it is applied; corporations, schools, colleges, marriages and families. Even after 56 years of marriage, we learned a great deal about each other and ourselves!"

JOHN AND ANN GIMENEZ · Founders of "Washington for Jesus" and Pastors, the Rock Church— "*Speaking of Love* is both thoughtful and educational. It will not only make you think, but it will also move you into action. The results can only be positive, whether for marriages, families or for your staff, departments and entire organization."

MIKE HAYES · **Senior Pastor** · **Covenant Church**— "Having known the Kendalls for 20 years, I commend them for their work with marriages, families, church staffs, corporations and organizations. Their utmost integrity has earned them a high level of respect among ministry peers and local and national leaders. Their understanding and experience in both corporate and church environments affords them tremendous insights into all levels of communication and relationships."

KAREN HAYTER · **Producer/Host, COPE, American Christian Television System (ACTS)**— "It was a joy to meet Fred and Anna and to explore the Seven Behavioral Life Languages and how to communicate love to each other. WOW! Did we learn a lot!"

MANNY HENDRIX · **Athletic Consultant** · **Former Professional Football Player for the Dallas Cowboys**— "The Seven Behavioral Life Languages restores a badly needed perspective of how to communicate effectively and openly. If this information is applied, your love will grow, your marriage flourish and success will chase you."

DR. CARLE M. HUNT · **Professor of Business**— "Fred is in a stage of leadership where his speaking and interpersonal skills are highly effective in both large and small groups. Right relationships, character development and open, honest communication are Fred's passions. And he models what he teaches. Plus, he has a gift to identify with his audience to motivate people to change."

DONNA JENKINS · **Assistant Director of Human Resources** · **City Government**— "The workshops provided by the Kendalls and Life Languages Institute, has, by far, been the best return on our training dollars invested in communication and team-building. They have profiled the languages of our Mayor, City Council, City's Director-level staff, supervisors, fire and police, secretaries, etc. Knowing our Life Languages, and those of our co-workers have helped all of us reach a clearer understanding of what is needed to work together and is a true enhancement of our commitment to appreciating diversity.

MARCIA AND JOHN KENDALL · **Ministry Director** · **700 Club, CBN**— "May we learn to express our languages as Fred and Anna have taught in this wonderful book, so our relationships are filled with such love, joy and peace that when one cries the other tastes the salt."

JACK KING · **Elder · Head of Men's Ministry**— "At the last Men's Retreat, we had many, many exciting testimonies how the power of Christ changed men's lives. Just two examples. In one situation, an individual had been close to taking the life of another man who had "stolen" then married his wife/ex-wife. Subsequently the latter got saved – then led the former to Christ. Today, both men are friends in the Lord. Another man suffered through the tragic suicide of his college age son. The Men's Retreat played a major role in helping heal his inner wounds. Fred's dynamic teaching, encouragement and positive affirmation was an important factor in reaching and touching men such as these."

FREDA LINDSAY · **Chairman of the Board and Co-founder of Christ For The Nations**— "I have known Fred and Anna Kendall for many years and have seen them bring help and hope to marriages and families. Their insights into different communication styles through the Seven Behavioral Life Languages is invaluable!"

DAVID C. MILLER · **Police Chief · City Government**— "The Kendalls have provided training for my department, and we have found it to be very useful in communication driven settings like problem solving, disciplinary recommendations, and career development, not to mention the routine of day to day office operations."

KEITH NELSON · **Board Certified Family Law Attorney**— "The Life Languages is an important seminar that will help strengthen communication between people, couples, clients and corporations. I recommend everyone read this book and attend one of these life changing seminars."

RANDY PARKER · **Executive Vice President · Loggins Meat Co., Inc.**— "Through attending the Kendall's seminar and then reading *Speaking of Love*, my wife and I were able to better understand the differences between our daughters, and sons-in-law, and ourselves. We now see that although we are different, we are each so special. I have also gained new understanding of my working relationships with those in my company."

CHERYL PREWITT SALEM · **Author, Recording Artist, Miss America 1980**— "The Kendall's book is a marriage study course that could change every marital, family and working relationship, if you will listen with your heart, mind and soul."

DAVID SHIBLEY · **President · Global Advance**— "This is a book every married couple should read to better understand each other, and a book that every person should read to better understand himself or herself."

Marjorie Slaten · School Counselor— "I have been using the Life Languages with troubled and at-risk students and their families. It is amazing how understanding these languages has opened them up. They are less judgmental, more accepting, and more supportive of one another. Now they show appreciation of their differences rather than teasing or attacking one another. It's bringing light where there once was confusion."

Don Spear · Certified Financial Planner · Spear Financial— "My wife Autumn and I have never read a book that is as enlightening as *Speaking of Love*. But best of all – it works! We recommend every family place this book on their list of priority reading. It also provides the key to cohesiveness and productivity in the workplace, and every corporation should bring the Kendalls in for a seminar."

Charles Stair · President and CEO ServiceMaster Management Services— "Learning the Seven Life Languages is extremely helpful to everyone for all relationships. I applaud your work."

Darlene Stout, BSN, CADAC, LCDC · Program Counselor · Baylor University Medical Center— "The Life Languages gives insightful, how-to information on communication that is totally 'user-friendly'. It is a wonderful tool for marriage and family therapy."

Herb Wheeler · Commanding Officer, Former Navy Aviator— "Having been shot down over Vietnam, I know that correct communication and understanding others can be the difference in life or death. The Seven Behavioral Life Languages can literally save your life, career, marriage and children."

John P. Wier, P.E., R.P.L.S. · President, Weir & Associates, Inc. (Engineering, Surveying, Land Planning)— "The Kendalls' workshop on the languages was presented in an open and honest, professional, businesslike, friendly and fun manner. All of our employees found the experience to be enjoyable and educational as they learned more about communicating and understanding."

Jim Witt · City Manager · City Government— "We have worked with the Kendalls and Life Languages Institute in an ongoing, comprehensive program to improve communication and understanding within our city government. We heartily recommend that organizations review this program and apply it to their management objectives and strategies."

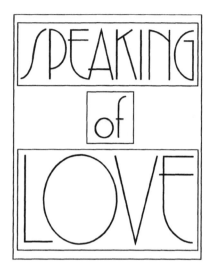

SPEAKING of LOVE

Fred and Anna Kendall
with
Mary Hollingsworth

Unless otherwise noted, Scripture quotations in this publication are from THE NEW KING
JAMES VERSION. Copyright © 1979, 1980, 1982, 1990, Thomas Nelson, Inc., Publishers.
Scripture quotations noted AMPLIFIED are from The Amplified Bible: Old Testament, copyright
© 1962, 1964 by Zondervan Publishing House (used by permission) and from The Amplified
New Testament, copyright © 1958 by the Lockman Foundation (used by permission).
Scripture quotations noted NRSV are from the New Revised Standard Version of the Bible.
Copyright © 1989 by the Division of Christian Education of the National Council of the
Churches of Christ in the United States of America.

Library of Congress Cataloging-in-Publication Data

Kendall, Fred, 1937–
    Speaking of love / Fred and Anna Kendall ; with Mary Hollingsworth.
      p.   cm.
    ISBN 0-7852-8154-1 (hardcover)
    1. Marriage—Religious aspects—Christianity. 2. Communication in marriage.
  I. Kendall, Anna, 1941– . II. Hollingsworth, Mary, 1947– . III. Title.
BV835.K46   1995
248.8'44—dc20   94-39428
                                                       CIP

Printed in the United States of America.

2 3 4 5 6 — 00 99 98 97 96 95

DEDICATION

This book is dedicated to Michael, our
delightful, unique, and wonderful son,
who has patiently taught us to listen,
grow, and change. Through learning to
relate to him and each other, we
developed these seven languages.
These languages continue to be
experienced in our family as we have been
blessed with our daughter-in-law, Anita,
who brings a new language into our lives.
Our prayer is that this book will be a
multigenerational blessing to all our
families as our children and
grandchildren live, laugh, learn, and
love fluently in seven beautiful,
biblical languages.

Contents

■

Acknowledgments

■

Our sincere thanks to the many churches and businesses through the years that have invited us to present seminars on love in many languages, especially to Mike and Kathy Hayes and Covenant Church, who gave us the support and opportunity to first teach and develop this concept in 1986.

Thanks to Michael and Anita Kendall for hours of testing, research, and computer input.

Thanks to Pat Monfrey and Catherine and Francis Galloway for providing the refuge of their peaceful retreatlike homes for the quiet times we needed for creativity.

Thanks to Don and Autumn Spear, Bill and Pat Kushnir, Doug and Sylvia Hellman, Dennis and Sue Brewer, Ron and Linda Gonzales, and Gene and Charlotte Weaver for years of prodding, encouraging, praying, and befriending us in the long hours of work.

Thanks to Dr. Kris Chesky for his valuable input on the "Language Discovery Quiz," plus hours of long discussion.

Thanks to Gloria Drass for her marvelous help in turning our piles of notes and papers into this finished book through artwork, typesetting, and insightful suggestions for its improvement.

We also appreciate the ministers, business leaders, psychiatrists, psychologists, therapists, and counselors who have validated the effectiveness of these languages in helping individuals, couples, families, and groups.

And thanks for the thousands of couples and individuals who have sat in on our seminars and have taken the "Language Discovery

Quiz," and for their testimonies about the benefits they have gained from learning to be multilingual.

Our fondest thanks to each of you without whose help this book would still be a dream.

Foreword

■

What could be more crucial to a family than understanding what each member is trying to say? Yet especially during disagreements, understanding is often so difficult that one member suspects another is speaking a different language, which is probably true. In fact, there might be more than two languages spoken in your family. If there is a teenager in your house, there is sure to be at least one additional unknown tongue.

Yes, family members are different, and they communicate differently. In *Speaking of Love*, Fred and Anna Kendall have identified seven languages of love spoken in families.

I know Fred and Anna well. They are well qualified to write this book. Anna has the equivalent of a doctorate in the languages of love. She must; who else can understand Fred? And I have seen Fred communicate psychological insights to couples and hospital staff in a simple, straightforward manner. I know from hearing Fred and Anna speak in their family seminars that they are experts at relating sound biblical and psychological truths in practical terms. *Speaking of Love* is further proof of that.

Reading this book and taking its Language Discovery Quiz will allow you to identify your own language and discern its strengths and vulnerabilities. This insight may result in you and your family learning to celebrate the differences among you rather than stare at one another in bewilderment.

The beauty of this book is that it not only identifies the traits of each language of love but also goes deeper to identify the characteristics of those who speak it. Each language reflects the thoughts and personality of the speaker. Through an awareness of what is meant by the words spoken in your family and the personality traits of the speakers, a fuller knowledge of one another is possible.

God said, "Therefore a man shall leave his father and mother and be joined to his wife, and they shall become one flesh" (Gen. 2:24). *Speaking of Love* will help you and your spouse become one and your whole family live in harmony.

Steven L. Schultz, M.D., Th.M.
Diplomate of the American Board of Psychiatry
and Neurology in Adult and Child Psychiatry

Introduction

∎

The word *communication* comes from the same root as *com munion*, which means "common union." To share a commoi love language is to have communion with that person. It is an inti mate and completing experience, similar to communion with God.

Peter Drucker, often called the father of American management claims that 80 percent of all management problems are a result o: faulty communications. Most leading marriage counselors say that al least 90 percent of all marital problems and divorces result from fault) communications between mates. Criminologists tell us that 90 per cent of all criminals have difficulty communicating with other people.

Have you ever felt as if you and your mate are speaking different languages when you try to communicate? No matter what you say or do, it seems your spouse takes it the wrong way? And it seems every time your mate says or does anything, it feels like an insult or a put-down?

Well, perhaps you *are* speaking different languages—one or more of the seven languages of love.

When God confused the language of the people on earth at the Tower of Babel, He did an almighty excellent job of it. We have always thought that confusion affected only the spoken language of the people and that the wave of His divine hand had simply shattered earthly communication into English, French, German, Spanish, and the like.

Although that is true, language is much more than mere words. How we communicate with each other involves words combined with sights, sounds, and actions; communication involves the entire behavioral style. So, when God confused people's language, He also confused their styles and manners of behavior, no doubt. And marriage is the primary place where that confusion can result in disaster.

Speaking of Love is the tool you need to rebuild any broken bridges of communication between you and your spouse. By identifying your behavioral language and then the language of your mate, you will open vistas of understanding you have never had before. Differences become celebrations instead of confrontations. Love becomes intimate and complete.

By using the "Language Discovery Quiz" in Part 2, you will be able to identify your and your mate's styles of communicating love (love languages). Then by studying the specific chapters that explain and explore these languages, you will be able to relate to your mate in caring and loving ways and vice versa.

There are at least seven ways of speaking of love. They are God-designed for exciting, lifelong marriages. Discover your unique language of love from God now by reading *Speaking of Love*. Then become fluent in the language of your mate, too. You will find a world of joy and love open to you as your marriage improves on all fronts.

This book is intended to be used as a learning tool first of all, then as a handy reference book. We want it to be a companion to your marriage, a friend, an interpreter. Enjoy it. Delight in it. Use it.

This book offers the information you have been looking for—it is the missing piece of your marriage puzzle. It can save your marriage, just as it has saved the marriages of many with whom we have shared it in counseling and seminars through the years. We pray your application of this information will bring your marriage joy, love, and intimacy.

FRED AND ANNA KENDALL

REAL LOVE IS THE UNIVERSAL LANGUAGE— UNDERSTOOD BY ALL.

∎

ARNOLD TOYNBEE

PART ONE

Marriage: Bliss or Miss?

■

IF I DO NOT KNOW
THE MEANING OF
THE LANGUAGE, I
SHALL BE A
FOREIGNER TO HIM
WHO SPEAKS, AND
HE WHO SPEAKS
WILL BE A
FOREIGNER TO ME.

■

1 CORINTHIANS 14:11

CHAPTER 1

Se Habla "Love"?

■

Act 1

Anna heard the snow whispering God's love to her as it softly disguised the barren winter earth with glistening purity. She felt the snow was her special gift from God this Christmas morning. She smiled as she watched the flakes blend into a quiet coverlet for her lawn. Christmas was her favorite day of the year, a day of giving and hospitality.

Glancing at the Christmas tree with its multicolored lights and silver icicles, she felt warm all over just thinking about the special presents she had so carefully chosen for her new husband, Fred. It was their first Christmas as husband and wife, and she was sure he would be as excited as she and her three-year-old son Michael were.

A second look at the presents, though, made her pause. Although there were gifts under the tree for Anna from friends, her family, and Fred's family, there were no gifts from Fred. Not even one. She decided he must be planning a really special surprise, waiting until the last minute to bring them all out, keeping her in suspense. She wondered what gift he would give her—something romantic perhaps? Or could it be something sentimental and sweet?

The coffee was ready. Anna put a big mug of the eye-opening liquid on the tray and stepped back. Perfect! The white linen cloth and napkin, the silver bud vase and red rose, his favorite eggs Benedict and bagel with cream cheese, sliced tomatoes, green chilies—everything was perfect. Carefully lifting the exquisite tray, she carried it down the hall to their bedroom where Fred was still sleeping. Breakfast in bed was the first of many surprises she had for Fred today.

"Merry Christmas, Darling!" Anna said as she gave Fred a passionate good morning kiss.

"Wow! What's all this?" asked Fred in disbelief, rubbing his eyes as he sat up.

"It's Christmas! And it's five o'clock in the morning. Wake up, you sleepyhead, and smell the coffee," bubbled Anna.

"You're bringing me breakfast in bed?" asked Fred. "This is totally out of character for you. You're never up first! What did I do to deserve this?"

"You married me. And today is Christmas. So, I thought I'd surprise you with breakfast in bed. It's my first present to you on our very first Christmas."

"Present?" asked Fred.

"Yes. Now, eat your breakfast so we can go open our other presents."

Anna talked happily about Christmas and the snow, while Fred quietly ate his breakfast. She wondered why he was so quiet, but she figured he was just not fully awake yet.

When Fred dusted off his mouth with the napkin for the last time, Anna set the tray aside and grabbed his hand, pulling him out of bed and down the hall to the living room. She could not wait any longer for the presents. She was like a little child expecting surprises from Santa Claus. Fred was still quiet.

"I'll go first," grinned Anna. Picking up one of the brightly wrapped packages, she sat on the floor by Fred's chair as he opened the present. Meanwhile, Michael was eagerly ripping open his gifts from Santa.

"A sweater. How nice," said Fred with little feeling. "I bet it will keep me warm, but do I really need another sweater and in pink?"

Undaunted, Anna continued to give Fred presents, until he had opened all of them. His response was less than gratifying. Then she waited. But Fred made no move to retrieve her gifts from wherever he had them hidden. So, she went on to their gifts from friends and family. When all were opened, Anna smiled at him and said, "Well? It's your turn."

"My turn? My turn for what?"

"Okay, Fred, stop teasing me. Where are my gifts? Are they hidden in the car? In the closet? In the garage?"

"No, they're not hidden," said Fred quietly.

"Well, then, where are they?"

"Uh, Anna, I didn't buy any presents."

"Right, Fred, you just forgot Christmas," laughed Anna. "Come on, now, where are they?" She was sure he was still kidding her. No one forgot Christmas. No one!

"Anna, I was so busy working and planning for next year that I didn't get around to it," he responded. "Just a minute." Fred got up and went to the bedroom. In a couple of minutes he came back and handed Anna a hundred-dollar bill. "Look, Honey, here's a hundred-dollar bill, and I'll give you another hundred dollars later. Besides you love to shop, and this way you can take in the after-Christmas sales and get exactly what you want." Thinking he had a logical answer to an emotional dilemma, he reached out to hug her and said, "Merry Christmas!"

Anna pushed his arms away in disbelief and said, "Are you telling me that you didn't get me even one Christmas gift? You really forgot Christmas?"

"Well, it sort of slipped up on me. Besides, I've never been very good at buying gifts," he admitted. "I love you, I'll always take care of you, and I don't mind how much you spend. Isn't that enough?"

"I can't believe you don't care enough to get me even one Christmas gift," said Anna as she began to cry.

"I do care, Anna. I love you very much." Fred reached out to touch her, but Anna pulled away, tears playing chase down her cheeks.

"Just leave me alone," she said, going to stare out the window at the snow.

"I'm sorry, Honey. Really I am. I've just never been good at remembering to buy gifts."

"Forget it," sobbed Anna loudly (partly because she was really hurt but also partly for the dramatic effect).

Bewildered at Anna's emotionalism over such a little thing, Fred went about his day filled with his usual projects, plans, and activities, thinking she would get over it before too long, especially when his family arrived. After all, that was the way his dad always handled Christmas gift giving, and Fred had learned it well. Anna went about the rest of Christmas Day determined to make the best of it, trying to act like nothing was wrong while Fred's family was there, but deep inside she was feeling confused and rejected. And she feared that Fred did not really love her.

Act 2

As the years of their marriage trudged by, Fred forgot birthdays, anniversaries, Mother's Day, Valentine's Day, and practically every other special date. He almost never bought gifts for Anna; each occasion seemed to come as a total surprise to him. If he did buy a gift, it was usually a last-minute dash into an appliance store for some unromantic, practical tool or to the drugstore for the wrong perfume. Anna became more and more frustrated by his lack of love. And he became more confused than ever about her overly emotional responses to such mundane events as holidays, birthdays, and anniversaries.

Anna tried everything to change or reform Fred into the thoughtful, giving husband she really wanted. She tried crying and pouting, which only left him angry and confused. Then she became creative by dropping hints and leaving newspaper or magazine ads of things she wanted lying around, which he rarely noticed. Finally, she told Fred outright when the important date was and what present she wanted, which he still often forgot.

Meanwhile, Anna could never quite keep up with the hectic pace of activities that Fred carefully planned for them. She missed appointments, was late to almost everything, and really did not seem to be concerned about her lack of punctuality. Fred was annoyed and frustrated. Why did Anna not care enough about him to at least be on time? She didn't seem to appreciate all the work he did to keep her life active, busy, and exciting.

Obviously, the marriage was doomed to fail.

Act 3: Years Later

One day Fred came home from the counseling office where he had been working with a couple whose marriage was coming apart. He was telling Anna about their conversation.

"Jane would say, 'Joe never tells me he loves me.' Then Joe would say, 'But I go out and work hard every day to make a home for her and take care of her. Isn't that love?' It was as if they were speaking two different languages, Anna. You should have heard them."

Pause. Anna looked at Fred. Fred looked at Anna. And realization streaked across both faces at once.

"That's it, Fred!" said Anna excitedly. "They *are* speaking different languages—languages of behavior. They are both expressing their love but in different ways. And neither one of them understands the other."

"That's right. They're really very much in love, but they don't know how to tell each other. It's as if one is speaking German and the other English."

"Say, that sounds like us, doesn't it?" asked Anna seriously.

Pause. Anna looked at Fred. Fred looked at Anna. And realization slapped them in the faces again.

"You really do love me, even though you don't express it with gifts, don't you, Fred?" asked Anna quietly.

"I love you more than anything in the world, Anna. And you love me, too, even though being on time is not important to you, don't you?"

"Of course I do, Honey."

Pause. We will skip the details about what happened next, but suffice it to say that this was the beginning of a new dimension of communication and understanding.

Epilogue: The Present

Anna stands looking out at the snow on Christmas morning. She smiles at the past and glances over at the glimmering Christmas lights and tinsel icicles on the tree. Under the tree are lots of presents. Some are from Anna to Fred, and several are from Fred to Anna.

Has Fred suddenly become a prolific gift giver? Not really, but he is working on it. When they finally identified their special-but-different God-given ways of loving, a new depth of understanding and communication was established, and Fred and Anna's marriage bonded for life. Now, when it is gift-giving time, Anna buys herself something really wonderful that she has been wanting. She wraps it up in gorgeous paper with a card that says, "From Fred to Anna with love."

When the time comes to open presents, Anna opens her gift. She is thrilled and truly pleased with the gift. And Fred watches her with delight, knowing he bought her something she really wanted.

One day Fred thrilled Anna by buying her a gift all by himself—
a white Maltese puppy. Named Samson in contrast to his tiny size,
he's a symbol of Fred's love for Anna and Anna's constant companion.

On the flip side, Anna has come to understand and appreciate
Fred for working so hard to organize his many activities and accomplishments and for providing a home for her and their son, Michael.
She has learned that his leadership and provision for them are his
way of loving them. So, she makes special efforts to be on time,
praise Fred for being such an excellent provider, and not miss
appointments.

Of course, that is not the whole story of their marriage. There
were a few other serious complications and adjustments before their
marriage became healthy and developed maturity. But their marriage began a major turnaround when they started understanding
the different languages of behavioral communication and applying
them to their relationship, as well as teaching them to others.

The God of Love

Love is the most important concept in the Bible because "God is
love" (1 John 4:8). To be like God, we must love, and married love is
the most intimate and fulfilling kind of love in the world.

> GOD IS THE GREAT CREATOR. JUST AS HE DID NOT
> CREATE ONLY ONE KIND OF ANIMAL, ONE COLOR OR
> FRAGRANCE OF FLOWERS, OR ONE RACE OF PEOPLE,
> NEITHER DID HE CREATE ONLY ONE WAY OF LOVING.
> THERE ARE, IN TRUTH, MANY DIFFERENT WAYS OF
> LOVING AND SPEAKING OF LOVE.

Each of us has a special way of loving that is given and appointed
to us by God Himself. It is natural. We do it without thinking. To us,
it seems the *only* way. And others know us by our unique way of giving and receiving love. Our behavioral style or love language does or
does not attract someone else to us. It is the essence of us.

Other people speak different love languages. Their languages,
too, are God-given and special. But to us, their ways of loving may

seem strange, and we often misinterpret them. To express love to each other in ways that can be understood and appreciated, we must learn to speak each other's languages of love. We must learn how God created our mates to love in order to relate to them successfully, especially within the private, intimate world of marriage.

What Did You Say?

A mature-looking woman went to an attorney and told her, "I want to divorce my husband."

The attorney asked, "Well, do you have any grounds?"

She answered, "Why, yes. We have almost an acre."

The puzzled attorney replied, "You don't understand. I want to know whether you and your husband have a grudge."

"Actually, we don't," she answered, "but we do have a nice carport."

"Okay, let's try something else. How are your sexual relations?"

The woman said, "Well, I guess they're all right. We haven't heard from any of them since the Fourth of July."

At this, the attorney shook her head and said, "I'm sorry, but I just don't see that any of this is a good enough reason for you to divorce your husband."

The woman looked at the attorney and said, "It's just that the man can't carry on an intelligent conversation."

That is the way some people communicate—or do not communicate.

Here is another example. A couple was driving down the street with the husband's eighty-seven-year-old mother in the car.

The wife was looking out the window. "It's windy," she said.

"No, it's Thursday," the husband corrected.

"I'm thirsty, too," said his mother. "Let's stop for something to drink."

That is just how confusing life can be when communication breaks down. It is like a meeting of the United Nations without interpreters.

We are reminded of the wonderful "I Love Lucy" television program. Lucy was married to Ricky Ricardo, a Cuban band leader, not too long off the boat from Cuba. Every time Lucy pulled one of her crazy stunts, Ricky would fly into a Cuban rage and begin ranting wildly in Spanish, which was his native language. He did not even realize he was speaking in a way Lucy could not understand. Lucy spoke no Spanish, of course, so she would cringe and hide her head until he finished waving his arms and yelling at her. Even though she did not understand his words, she knew he was angry. Their friends, Fred and Ethel, would stand by in silence watching the comical display. When Ricky had finished his entire speech in Spanish, Lucy would calmly say, "Not that we really want to know, but would you mind repeating that in English so the rest of us can understand you?"

The "I Love Lucy" show was funny and highly successful. One reason was the constant lack of communication between marriage partners that the show's writers played up in the script. American couples related to that failure to communicate even subconsciously. We saw ourselves in Lucy and Ricky. Although our human languages are not necessarily culturally different, often our communication styles are very different. And the result is the same as Lucy and Ricky's—chaos, confusion, out-of-control situations—but it is *not* funny. It is painful and destructive, and marriages often dissolve in the acid created.

Defining Language

Language is not just words, as Ricky and Lucy demonstrate. To a deaf person, language is sight and hand signs that sing of love through the silence. To a blind person, language is sounds of love that illuminate the lonely darkness. To Helen Keller, who was both blind and deaf, language was the caring touch of her teacher, Anne Sullivan. To a baby, language is hugging, holding, feeding when hungry, and changing a wet diaper.

Around the world, language is a full spectrum of communication elements specialized for each culture. It includes words, all right, and so much more! Language is a combination of sounds, sights, tastes, smells, touch, writing or drawing, time, light, space, feelings, and actions. It is behavioral patterns, body postures and movement, and unspoken-but-meaningful glances or glares.

BY LANGUAGE, IN ALL ITS FACETS, PEOPLE LIVE IN
PEACE OR GO TO WAR. THEY SING HYMNS IN
HARMONY OR SHOUT INSULTS. THEY EXPRESS LOVE
OR HATRED. WITHIN THE INTIMATE WORLD OF
MARRIAGE, LANGUAGE IN ALL ITS FACETS IS HOW
COUPLES LIVE TOGETHER IN PEACE OR PAIN.

Communicate or Die

Captain Eugene "Red" McDaniel, a navy pilot, was shot down in
North Vietnam and held as a prisoner of war for six years. In his
book *Scars and Stripes,* he described the desperate need of prisoners
to communicate with one another to maintain morale. He said that
POWs tended to die much sooner if they could not communicate.

On many occasions Captain McDaniel endured torture rather
than give up his attempts to stay in touch with other prisoners, especially when he was in solitary confinement. Prisoners risked death to
work out a complicated communications system where they wrote
under plates, coughed, sang, tapped on walls, laughed, scratched,
spat, or flapped laundry a certain number of times to transmit a let-
ter of the alphabet.

"One thing I knew," says McDaniel, "was that I had to have
communication with my own people. Like me, they wanted to live
through it, if at all possible. Communication with each other was
what the North Vietnamese captors took the greatest pains to prevent. They knew, as well as we did, that a person can stand more pain
if linked with others of his own kind in that suffering. The lone, isolated person becomes weak and vulnerable. I knew I had to make
contact, no matter what the cost."

FOR THOSE BRAVE MEN, IT WAS COMMUNICATE OR
DIE. AND FOR MARRIAGE, IT IS COMMUNICATE OR
WATCH YOUR MARRIAGE DIE A CRUEL DEATH—THE
DEATH OF DISCONNECTEDNESS, THE DEATH OF
NEGLECT, THE STONE-SILENT DEATH OF APATHY.

In this book, the word *language* encompasses all its facets. A love language includes words and actions. It includes behavioral patterns and methods of communicating love. Language is a full-spectrum concept.

Just as learning to speak a foreign language opens up new geographical, cultural, and political communications, learning to speak your mate's language of love opens up new worlds of communication and intimacy in marriage.

In counseling married couples and individuals in our Family Restoration Network, we have seen that communication breaks down on many different levels. A primary breakdown is how people show and perceive love. For example, a wife says that she does not feel loved because her husband does not spend enough time with her. He says, "Of course I love her, and I tell her several times a day. And she's sure a fine one to complain. She never tells me she loves me unless I force it out of her."

They are speaking two different love languages, and neither of them understands how love is being shown by the other. For example, she feels truly loved and appreciated only when he shares significant time with her. He feels loved when she tells him she loves him. He speaks his language to her, but she fails to understand and receive it because he did not spend enough quality time as an expression of love. She arranges her work so that when they are together everything is finished that would take her time or attention away from him. She can then sit quietly by his side for hours at a time, showing him she loves him, but he does not receive the message because she did not state her love to him. The truth is, they love each other deeply, but neither one experiences the assurance of that love because they have a love language barrier.

What's the solution? It is the same solution for overcoming any language barrier. By learning to understand and speak each other's language, the barrier is torn down, and the love can be understood.

Action/Response

EXPRESSING

Love is both proactive and responsive. Via your special style of communicating love, you are constantly sending out (expressing) and receiving messages of love. The information in this book will help you send out your messages of love in seven different languages, as figure 1.1 shows.

Fig. 1.1. Expressing Messages

In addition, this book will enable you to tune your receiver to accept incoming messages of love in seven different languages, as shown in figure 1.2.

Majors and Minors

Each of us has been given one primary, or major, love language. Usually, we also have one or two secondary, or minor, languages. It is like college where you may have graduated with one major degree in education and two minor degrees in English and Bible. You may then have several other areas of study in which you have lesser abilities, such as math or history. Perhaps you can do some bookkeeping, but your checkbook may not always be in balance. Or maybe you enjoy reading history, but you cannot remember all those dates.

Fig. 1.2. Receiving Messages

The love languages operate in much the same way. You have one primary language that is natural and easy for you. Then you probably also have one or two secondary languages in which you have some fluency. Although you will likely never function fluently in all seven love languages, you can learn to identify and recognize them in order to communicate well enough to make others feel significant and loved.

The reason to learn the languages of love is not to label or limit you or your mate; it is to help you connect and communicate with him or her.

The Challenge

Marriage can become sick on various levels, but poor communication is usually the fatal malady. The lines of communication become broken, like snow-weighted telephone lines in a storm. Sometimes, through lack of attention, the lines are never repaired. Sometimes lack of knowledge about how to repair the broken lines perpetuates and extends the problem.

No matter what state your marriage is in right now, from seemingly hopeless to hallelujah, the insights in this book can bring to your marriage a new excitement of learning and growing together. Share the adventure of learning to say "I love you" in the language your mate best understands. Learning to speak your mate's language is a dynamic demonstration of your love. Refusing to learn that language is a demonstration of selfishness and apathy toward your mate and your marriage. Reach out in the many languages of love.

A GOOD MARRIAGE IS THE PEACEFUL COEXISTENCE OF TWO NERVOUS SYSTEMS.

—EMIL KROTKY

PART TWO

The Seven Languages of Love: An Exploration and Explanation

■

**TEST YOURSELVES.
DO YOU NOT KNOW
YOURSELVES, THAT
JESUS CHRIST IS IN
YOU?**

■

2 CORINTHIANS 13:5

CHAPTER 2

What Love Languages Do You Speak?

HOW TO TAKE THE LIFE LANGUAGES PROFILE

■

This is the third edition (and first paperback edition) of our book, *Speaking of Love*. Chapter Two and Three are revisions, and the Addendum at the end of the book introduces the 115 question Kendall Life Language Profile (or KLLP) and four sets of Answer Sheets. There are also seven new, descriptive, icons, one for each language. These are additions to the original hardback book published by Thomas Nelson.

Discovery is both fun and challenging, It's fun to discover something you want to know about yourself – something positive and encouraging. And it's challenging to find areas where you still have room for growth. How do you discover your primary Behavioral Life Language? The most accurate way is to stop right now and tear out the answer sheets in the back of the book. You, your mate, (and you may also give the KLLP to your children over thirteen) get comfortable, answer the KLLP and mail your answers to the address as shown. In just a few days you will each receive your own personal computer printout. (More about the printout in a moment . . .)

Then continue reading and learning about yourself and the Life Languages and let each chapter be a workbook. As you discover positives and negatives check off those like you or your spouse. Make your check marks in different colored ink and at the end of each chapter, total your check marks. The chapter with the most check marks will probably be your primary language. The tricky part is determining your second, third, fourth, fifth, sixth and seventh languages. When your computer printout arrives, you will enjoy comparing it to your check marks.

Discovering more about yourself and your mate is an enjoyable experience. All languages and all combinations of languages are good, and can be compatible with one another. This is why we believe that all marriages can work with understanding and good communication. Every language is designed by God for His own excellent purpose. Enjoy discovering which of God's languages He has appointed for you, and seek to understand that language. Then, as you learn to speak and understand the other languages you will become multilingual.

To really love others and build lasting relationships, you need to grow through learning their communication styles and adapting your behavior to their needs. Love is the ability to communicate understanding and meaning to your spouse. *Speaking of Love* and the Kendall Life Language Profile will help you to acquire the knowledge, vision and destiny to become a better friend and lover to your spouse. The potential is exciting!

We are sometimes asked, "Are the Seven Behavioral Life Languages personality traits or spiritual gifts?" Our opinion is that they are both.

Biblically, we understand that there are three types of gifts that relate directly to God: as the Father, the Son and the Holy Spirit.

The nine gifts from the Holy Spirit for the believer are the gifts named in I Corinthians 12:7-12. The purpose of these gifts is to strengthen the Church as well as comfort, equip and empower the believer.

The five gifts from Jesus are found in Ephesians 4:7-16 and establish roles, purposes or ministry of those who serve the Church and the Body of Christ. Redemptively, Jesus gives us His greatest gift – the gift of eternal life through his shed blood.

The seven gifts from the Father, as described in Romans 12:3-8, are often called the motivations, traits or tendencies that characterize each person through the Creator's unique workmanship in us. All of us are created in the Father's Image and we believe that all of us receive one primary, motivational or functional gift from the Father that manifests through our personality and aptitude. Then we have lesser degrees of the other functional gifts. These functional gifts provide the framework around which the basic personality develops. Before you were born-again, your motivational gifts provided a semi-latent structure for your basic personality. After you were born-again, they became empowered by the spirit of God. As you grow spiritually and increasingly abandon yourself to God, your gifts further develop and blossom. They yield fruit that is reflected in the fullness of your personality. When you reach a relatively high level of spiritual development, other gifts that were less dominant begin to show up as well. Ultimately, you will discover that all of God's functional or motivational gifts become so evident in your attitudes and behavior that neither your carnal nature nor your past experiences have power over you any longer. Instead of being bound by the past, you are set free to live abundantly in the present.

It is our experience and opinion that the gifts of the Father named in Romans 12:3-8 correlate with our Seven Behavioral Life Languages. The more spiritually mature we become, and the more yielded to the Father, the more multi-lingual we become. We believe that Jesus manifested all the gifts and that he was, therefore, multi-lingual. And since Jesus lives in us, we can be multi-lingual! Then we desire to learn to speak the languages of those we are in relationship with. We get excited about understanding them and showing them love. And the greatest way to show someone your love and God's love, is to show it in the Behavioral Life Language that they speak!!!

In profiling large numbers of people within both Christian and secular communities, we get the same experimental and empirical results. We have been researching, testing, studying, applying and sharing these Life Languages since 1986, but we believe they can be traced back to the apostle Paul around 53-56 A.D.

We continue to learn and refine the Seven Behavioral Life Languages, and are delighted to bring you our updated discoveries. It is our experience that anyone who studies and applies the languages for three years, has them for life. You will find relationships improve, including your relationship with the Father and yourself.

Since 1986, thousands of individuals, couples, families and businesses around the United States have taken variations of the Kendall Life Language Profile. We have conducted seminars and workshops in churches, counseling centers, governmental agencies, colleges, corporations and psychiatric hospitals. The KLLP has been subjected to considerable technical and market research analyses. We have consulted with various experts in the areas of programming, psychology, education, testing and measurements and have been greatly enriched by their abundance of statistical analysis and guidance. We have also received input from pastors across the country. The end result of all the consulting, analysis and research is the KLLP — a testing instrument that can determine a person's strengths, weaknesses, uniqueness and communication style through the seven Behavioral Life Languages.

Those who have taken the KLLP agree that it is an accurate and user-friendly instrument. We asked people who represent a cross section of the American population what they thought about the KLLP. To our delight, the results were overwhelmingly positive. Ninety-eight percent said the KLLP was easy to read, ninety-six percent said it was easy to understand and ninety-seven percent said it accurately pegged them!

WE HOPE YOU WILL AGREE WITH US THAT IN STUDYING PERSONAL-ITY TYPES, COMMUNICATION STYLES OR THE SEVEN BEHAVIORAL LIFE LANGUAGES, THE GOAL IS NOT GREATER SELF-CENTEREDNESS, BUT GREATER SELF THROUGH CHRIST-CENTEREDNESS.

The self is the person you were created to become when you were conceived, and God says in Isaiah 44: 1-4 that you are of great worth: "... I have called you by your name, you are Mine! ... You are precious in My sight". So He is telling us not to dislike ourselves. We are also told that it is a sin to be prideful. We cannot take credit for what or who we are, as it is God who makes us significant.

Self-centeredness is the stage when we are immature – where we think the world centers around us, our way, our pleasures and happiness, and selfish fulfillment is our highest priority. This is the condition without Christ, or the spiritually immature.

Spiritual maturity brings us to the level where the Lord wants us, and that is to come out of self-centeredness and into "self-sacrificing" – where we know who we are in Christ and we desire to emulate Him.

LET NOTHING BE DONE THROUGH SELFISH AMBITION OR CONCEIT, BUT IN LOWLINESS OF MIND LET EACH ESTEEM OTHERS BETTER THAN HIMSELF. LET EACH OF YOU LOOK OUT NOT ONLY FOR HIS OWN INTERESTS, BUT ALSO FOR THE INTERESTS OF OTHERS.

(PHIL. 2:3-4)

Learning your Life Languages and those of your mate will help you to see how fearfully and wonderfully you are made and how precious and valuable you are to God. Understanding our value helps us to move out of self-centeredness into self-sacrifice and Christ-centeredness.

In His Image/My Image, Josh McDowell tells of the importance of good self-esteem when he wrote:

"If you see yourself as a failure, you will find some way to fail, no matter how hard you want to succeed. On the other hand, if you see yourself as adequate and capable, you'll face life with more optimism and perform nearer your best."

As husbands and wives you play a big part in helping one another to see yourselves as capable and valuable. As you express love in one another's languages you are reinforcing God's love and providing the soil that will bring forth good fruit. Showing His love, using His gifts, for His purposes is the essence of a mature marriage.

And now as promised . . . more about what you will get in your personal, KLLP computer printout. The following explanation may sound somewhat technical, but don't let that concern you. Just be assured that you and your spouse will receive valuable information about yourselves, and that information will help you both to continue to become all that God created you to be. Therefore your marriage and your children will be the beneficiaries of your growth!

THE KENDALL LIFE LANGUAGES PROFILE™ (KLLP)

The Electronically scored KLLP – quantifies, qualifies and provides over 32 key foundational points of information on how an individual, group or corporation communicates. The seven Behavioral Life Languages are scored, rank-ordered from strongest to weakest, graphed and explained. In addition to the seven Behavioral Life Languages and the three categories, you will receive information on your:

Range – This is the distance between your Primary (or strongest) Behavioral Life Language and your weakest (or seventh) Life Language, as well as the distance between each Language. A high or low score is neither better nor worse, though very important. A high range means you tend to stand out in your primary language, and your behavior is therefore more definable. However, you may have more difficulty communicating with those who speak your weaker languages. A low range means you tend to communicate easily with all the languages, but you may be less predictable and understandable to others. The failure to understand range is one of the primary cause of communication difficulties.

Intensity – The Intensity score reveals the strength, energy and passion shown in communication. A high or low score is neither better nor worse, though very meaningful. Once you understand Intensity, your chance for success in personal as well as professional relationships is greatly enhanced. This measurement explains reasons why one might be prone to conflict, or why one might sometimes or often be overlooked. By developing an awareness of your Intensity Level you can choose to increase your Intensity when needed or choose to control it to avoid conflict.

Filter – Each language has a filter that screens incoming communication, which determines the receiver's response or reaction. Failure to properly perceive your Filter is tantamount to rejection, confusion and ultimately failure.

Major Characteristics and Professions – The major characteristics of your primary Life Language provide insightful and valuable information for personal application. The propensity toward certain professions is useful in directing, motivating, and understanding yourself and others. The printout gives the professions in which those who speak your primary Life Language have been found to succeed and enjoy.

Positive and Negative Attributes – These attributes are covered in detail. Knowing your attributes will help you minimize or even eliminate any negative, destructive behavior that will sabotage relationships.

Descending Distress Levels – This knowledge can become the critical difference between success or failure during troubled, stressful times, and can even be life-saving. Learning to recognize and interdict this behavior in yourself and others can lead to less striving and more thriving.

Success Trait – Due to the nature of your profile, this missing trait or character quality must be developed for you to succeed and maintain success.

Major Desire – The major desire of each language is the primary motivation that directs your overall personality. Knowing this will increase contentment within interpersonal relationships, as well as increase job satisfaction.

Need from Others – Each person has needs that are met through other relationships and within each Life Language. This need is defined. When this need is met, we experience joy, love, and contentment. As we understand ourselves and others, we know how to get our needs met and be the instrument of meeting the needs of others. In corporate and sales situations, understanding the needs of others helps us to motivate them positively and result in reduction in turnover, absenteeism, conflicts, lost customers and missed sales.

Personal Habit – Each Life Language has a specific action that must be developed until it becomes a habit. This habit is a foundational key that leads to success.

When you receive your KLLP personalized printout, possibly for the first time in your life, you will get a healthy, balanced perspective on your past, and a keen, clear vision for your future. You will be surprised how many things and relationships start falling into place, once you see your-self more clearly.

All of us speak all seven of the Life Languages already. This is why you will find some part of each language that you can identify with. How-ever, we may focus on more of the negative characteristics than the posi-tive. Or our fluency may be stronger in one or two of the languages, and the others we barely recognize. That is why the KLLP can be so beneficial. As you learn to understand yourself and your spouse, and learn to speak the language of your spouse and others, you will see amazing things begin to happen.

AFTER YEARS OF COUNSELING APPROXIMATELY 10,000 MARRIED COUPLES AND FAMILIES, WE ARE CONVINCED THAT MOST OF US SIMPLY NEED TO SEE ONE ANOTHER AS GOD SEES US, EACH WITH OUR OWN UNIQUE NEEDS, ABILITIES AND TALENTS.

Seeing another as Christ does will cause us to celebrate and rejoice over their uniqueness and pray for their shortcomings. When we see each other through God's eyes, which are eyes of faith and potential, we help each other grow into that potential because faith is a creative force. One of the great purposes of marriage is to help one another overcome, heal and develop into a mature and precious child of God. This is a process which happens through love, and this book will give you practical ways to love one another.

The Gallop Poll and other such organizations have found that, in most cases, there is no significant difference between the behavior of the churched and the unchurched. In some situations the churched were even more likely to fail when tested and tempted in moral, ethical and legal matters. We know this to be a complex matter. However, we believe a starting place to reverse this confusing reality is for you to discover the imprint of character and aptitude given to you by God the Father. Dedi-cate time and effort to operating in the positives of your primary language, then one by one, the other six. Then couples in the secular community will have a biblical example of the value, profitability, joy and advantage of the Christian faith. You, by being further transformed into the image of Christ, will provoke the non-believer into desiring to be like you, which will lead them to Him.

We hope you will send off for your personal profile. (There is a charge for each profile, but we believe that you, your marriage and your family are worth investing in. You will receive a refund if you are not satisfied.) Regardless, we are confident that *Speaking of Love* is the beginning of a wonderful, transforming journey. Our prayer is that you will enjoy the journey as you travel the road to loving one another by becoming multilingual!

We, being many, are one body in Christ, and individually members of one another. Having then gifts differing according to the grace that is given to us, let us use them: if prophecy, let us prophesy in proportion to our faith; or ministry, let us use it in our ministering; he who teaches, in teaching; he who exhorts, in exhortation; he who gives, with liberality; he who leads, with diligence; he who shows mercy, with cheerfulness.

■

Romans 12:5–8

CHAPTER 3

What Did You Say, Honey?

AN OVERVIEW OF THE SEVEN LANGUAGES

■

N
ow we will explore and explain the seven different Behavioral Life Languages of love in detail. Here is where the fun begins. The fun part of each language is discovering the potential and power of your personal communication style when it is properly used within its godly limits. The part of each language that may need improvement comes into focus when you discover the danger and devastation that can occur when your communication style is out of God's control.

Study closely the chapters that deal with your primary and your two secondary languages. Learn as much about yourself and the way God created you to communicate as possible. Then also study the primary and secondary languages of your mate. Armed with the knowledge you will gain from this material, you will be able to fit the missing pieces into your marriage puzzle for a better relationship.

This short chapter is a quick reference overview of all seven languages. Use it often to verify the language traits you see in action around you. Study it carefully until you have it committed to memory. Share it with others. For instance, help your mate understand his or her own communication style as well as yours, thus doubling the improvement in your relationship.

As a starting place, please consider carefully the following scripture as it relates to the Dos and Don'ts: *"Who is the man who desires life, and loves many days, that he may see good? Keep your tongue from evil and lips from speaking deceit. Depart from evil and do good; seek peace and pursue it."* (Psalm 34:12-14)

Dos and Don'ts of the Seven Languages

Do

1. Accept that your language contributes to your uniqueness and is part of your specialness.

2. Accept the other person's language as God-appointed and God-designed.

3. Recognize that another behavioral language is as valid as your own.

4. Try to learn how to communicate with all the other languages effectively.

5. Help others to identify your language and learn how to communicate with you when they ask.

6. Celebrate and explore the differences and similarities of your language and your mate's. Remember that uniqueness and individualness are limitless and are a reflection of God's greatness.

7. Purpose to strengthen, be sensitive, learn to communicate effectively, regularly, and healthily in the languages in which you are weak.

Don't

1. Compare your language to others and feel that your or other languages are superior.

2. Try to change the person who speaks a language other than yours. God created him or her that way on purpose.

3. Criticize the characteristics of another language. Your language has negative traits as well.

4. Insist that your mate learn your language instead of your learning his or hers.

5. Limit yourself, your mate, or others through language labeling. Labeling is limiting and creates bondage, but through Jesus Christ we are set free!

6. Give up on learning your mate's behavioral style. Patience and persistence will pay off in the long run. Marriage is for life. Relationships in and through Christ are eternal.

7. Boast and label yourself in strong languages, and say, "That is just how we Doers are," or excuse and avoid responsibility because you are weak in certain languages. BECOME MULTILINGUAL.

Quick Reference Section

EMOTIVE LANGUAGES

 RESPONDER: Compassionate, Passionate, Sensitive, Warm, Reactive and Verbal

 INFLUENCER: Creative, Optimistic, Relational, Persuasive, Enthusiastic and Verbal

COGNITIVE LANGUAGES

 SHAPER/STRATEGIST: Organized, Visionary, Focused, Delegating, Strategic and Efficient

 CONTEMPLATOR: Inquisitive, Reflective, Sensitive, Peaceful, Calm and Complex

 PRODUCER/GIVER: Gracious, Responsible, Philanthropic, Resourceful, Thoughtful and Hospitable

KINETIC LANGUAGES

 MOVER: Direct, Assertive, Ambitious, Pioneering, Reactive and Standard Bearers

 DOER: Dedicated, Observant, Diligent, Practical, Efficient and Responsible

Please note: We have changed the names of "Strategist" to "Shaper" because they "Shape" their environment, and one of the ways they do that is by their strategic thinking. We have also changed the name of "Giver" to "Producer" because while they give in a philanthropic and cognitive way, other languages also give either through emotions or by actions. Our focus groups have confirmed that the new names are more inclusive of the full meaning of these two languages. These changes show up only in the icons and the printout at this time and not throughout the chapters.

Speaking of Love: The Seven Behavioral Languages

CATEGORY	"EMOTIVE" (Emotional)		"COGNITIVE" (Thinking)
LANGUAGES	RESPONDER	INFLUENCER	STRATEGIST
THREE MAJOR CHARACTER DESCRIPTIONS:	Compassionate, Sensitive, Warm	Creative, Optimistic, Relational	Organized, Visionary, Focused
RESPONDS TO LIFE IN THIS ORDER:	Feel . . . Act/Think	Feel/Think . . . Act	Think . . . Act . . . Feel
NEEDS FROM MATE:	*AFFECTION* and UNCONDITIONAL ACCEPTANCE along with hugs and a nurturing environment. Share your feelings and listen to theirs.	*AFFIRMATION* THROUGH WORDS of love, encouragement, inclusiveness, humor, and playfulness. Emotional connectiveness and reassurance of how important they are to you.	*AGREEMENT* and SUPPORT in THINKING process, planning, goals, vision, life purpose. Be sure to follow through on tasks assigned to you with both reporting details and accomplishments.
THE THREE LEVELS OF DISTRESS AND WARNING SIGNALS:	1. Over-pleases, denigrates self, pouts. 2. Feels confused, goes into denial, becomes defensive. 3. Acts out self-doubt. Feels rejected and unloved. Sinks into depression, bitterness, and unforgiveness. May seek relief through addictions and/or suicide.	1. Exaggerates, manipulates and controls others by over-talking and advising. 2. Defensive, gives formulas and goes into denial. 3. Feels rejected, unloved, and trapped, and moves into destructive behavior. May become verbally abusive and may move into addictive behavior.	1. Over-delegates or will do it all himself. Demanding, drives self and others harder. Cold and indifferent. 2. Uses people, sarcastic, critical, calloused. 3. Suspicious, won't trust, withdraws, isolates. Cuts everyone off. Runs away. May become addicted to uppers or exercise.

"COGNITIVE" (Thinking)		"KINETIC" (Action)	
CONTEMPLATOR	GIVER	MOVER	DOER
Studious, Reflective, Peaceful	Generous, Thoughtful, Responsible	Direct, Assertive, Standard Bearer	Dedicated, Observant, Conscientious
Think/Feel . . . Act	Think . . . Feel/Act	Act/Feel . . . Think	Act . . . Think . . . Feel
ATTENTION and QUALITY TIME when they want it, then give them their privacy and space needs when they want that.	**APPRECIATION** and THOUGHTFUL GIFTS for no reason and for all occasions. Graciousness and hospitality. Wise use of money and other resources.	**ACTION** - they need your response THROUGH ACTION. Also "do" things for them, and exciting things with them. Your attitude and actions must be congruent, honest, and complimentary.	**APPROVAL** of THEIR DEEDS. Say and do things that show your approval of their contribution. Do things for and with them.
1. Becomes prideful, inflexible, legalistic. 2. Critical, denies, defensive. 3. Feels rejected and unloved or goes to other extreme and feels smothered. Pushes others away. Withdraws and may abuse by isolating.	1. Becomes critical, materialistic, uses people. 2. Judgmental, controls others through money, bribes, "strings attached." 3. Becomes stingy, selfish, prideful, and more controlling. Buys way out of responsibility. Emotionally may become abusive.	1. Demanding, over-controlling, judgmental, blaming. 2. Resentful, caustic, attacks character of others. 3. Hostile, bitter, contemptuous. "Risk it all" behavior on big deals or "risk taking" hobbies and activities. Anger, may be physically abusive.	1. Expects perfection of self and others. Judgmental, blames. Over-works and organizes. 2. Becomes martyred. Broods, is resentful. 3. Depression, self-pity, accuses and rejects others. Anger turns to alienation, then to abuse. May be emotionally or physically abusive.

The Seven Behavioral Languages

They are divided into three categories:

1. Emotive (feelings)
2. Cognitive (thinking)
3. Kinetic (action)

1. The two emotive languages:
   a. Responder   b. Influencer

2. The three cognitive languages:
   a. Strategist   b. Contemplator   c. Giver

3. The two kinetic languages:
   a. Mover   b. Doer

The Two Emotive Languages

Responders are compassionate, sensitive, and warm, among other things:

- Feeling oriented
- Emotional
- Usually creative or artistic
- Sympathetic
- Affectionate (hug other people freely)
- People oriented
- Not aware of, or controlled by, time
- Very here and now oriented
- Usually very verbal

When talking to others, Responders touch their arms or hands, pat their backs or shoulders. They prefer small groups, and they have many friends.

Responders feel loved when they receive unconditional acceptance and affection and are hugged and touched often. They need to be shown affection; be sensitive and understanding to their emotional needs. Share your feelings with them, and encourage them to share their feelings with you in an accepting and nonjudgmental way to help Responders experience the true depth of your love.

Influencers are creative, optimistic, and relational, among other things:

- Highly verbal
- Encouraging
- Positive and optimistic
- Persuasive
- Talkative
- Enthusiastic
- Innovative
- People oriented
- Future oriented
- Solution oriented (rather than problem focused)

Influencers often speak before thinking. They like to move on to new projects and ideas. They enjoy groups of all sizes and have many friendships on all levels.

Influencers feel loved when they receive words of affirmation, when you say, "I love you." Verbal interaction is highly important to the feeling of love for Influencers. They enjoy talking about the activities of the day and about the future. Believe in Influencers; offer positive motivation, and express support.

The Three Cognitive Languages

Strategists are organized, visionary, and focused, among other things:

- Concerned about end results (will sacrifice short-range gratification or relationships for long-range goals)
- Advance planners (plan this year, next year, five years, and even ten years ahead)
- Efficient
- Accomplishment, rather than activity, oriented
- List makers
- People oriented
- Action oriented

Strategists can be at ease when under someone else's authority as well as have people under their authority. They are natural leaders. They are good managers of people, places, equipment, and things. They can manage large groups of people but socially enjoy small groups. They have only a few close friends.

Strategists feel loved through agreement and when you fit into and share their vision and plans. Participate with Strategists and they will feel loved. Well-thought-out actions are important to Strategists; show your love by thinking before you act around them. They will best understand carefully planned and executed expressions of love.

Contemplators are studious, reflective, and peaceful, among other things:

- Reasoning, logic, and process oriented
- Very loyal
- Thorough researchers of new ideas
- Good listeners
- Thinkers (think before speaking, think before acting, think through decisions carefully, even insignificant ones)

Contemplators guard their time and space. They have well-defined boundaries. They like to do one project at a time. They may be well informed but will not compete to talk about what they know. They usually have a few close friends that they tend to keep for life.

Contemplators feel loved when you give them undivided attention—when you carefully plan and set aside time with them with no interruptions or distractions. Contemplators feel loved when you listen patiently without advising as they work through thoughts and ideas. They feel loved when you share time with them, enjoying silence as well as talking. Contemplators need for you to respect the times when they need to be alone and to have uninvaded space.

Givers are generous, thoughtful, and responsible, among other things:

- Good-to-excellent money managers
- Surprise planners
- Good stewards of possessions
- Gracious and gifted at entertaining; hospitable

Givers prepare by planning and gathering ahead of time. They are always ready. They like to meet material needs of others. They make others feel special in their homes or offices. They entertain with ease and flair. They enjoy large or small groups, and they usually enjoy many friends.

Givers feel loved when they receive appreciation and thoughtfully given gifts for special occasions or for no reason at all. Share hospitality with Givers, or assist in being hospitable. Appreciate their making your home so warm, enjoyable, and hospitable.

The Two Kinetic Languages

Movers are direct, assertive standard bearers, among other things:

- Proactive people (forward thinking and acting)
- Action/result oriented
- Risk takers (not afraid of changes)
- Like excitement
- Strong personal standards and convictions of what is right
- Very honest and straightforward
- Concerned with motives of self and others
- High energy
- Innovators; leaders; visionaries
- Oftentimes dramatic

Movers enjoy small or large groups, and they usually have many acquaintances but few close friends. Movers may have just one or two real friends.

Movers feel loved when you do things with and for them—when action takes place for them. Movers want to know that the acts done are from a heart of commitment. The motive behind the action is as important to Movers as the action itself. Movers also feel loved when they are accepted.

Doers are dedicated, observant, and conscientious, among other things:

- Action oriented
- Responsive to what is happening (do not necessarily *make* things happen)
- Very now oriented
- Good maintainers
- Perception of physical and practical needs rather than psychological or spiritual needs
- Little time spent on personal introspection

- Great at following orders and assisting to bring tasks to completion
- Occupied with projects and activities

Doers like for their spouses to join in working on projects or activities. If they cannot do them together, Doers like for their spouses to be doing things on their own. Doers find a need and fill it. They are usually high-energy people. They enjoy small or large groups. They have many casual friends but not many close or intimate friends.

Doers feel loved when action is done *for* them or *with* them. The motive behind the action is not necessarily important; Doers feel loved just by having the things done. Having the car washed, food prepared, the lawn mowed, and shirts ironed are all expressions of love to Doers. All people like to feel noticed and appreciated, but Doers especially have this need. Almost all Doers protest being complimented or recognized for their deeds and contributions, but an unnoticed Doer is an unhappy Doer!

Emotive Languages
The Feelers

- ## The Responder
  ### Ephesians 5:2

- ## The Influencer
  ### Acts 4:20

People who speak emotive languages generally respond to life, people, and values first with their hearts, then with their heads and actions.

Individuals who speak emotive languages are *people* people. They are energized and fulfilled by their relationships and interactions with others. People who speak other languages are attracted and naturally drawn to people who speak emotive languages.

Examples of persons in this language category would be Mother Teresa, who has ministered to a generation of people, to Saint Francis of Assisi, who loved and cared for all living things including the smallest animals. Their lives revolve around caring for, being with, connecting with, and touching the lives of others.

Responder

Compassionate

Sensitive

Warm

*Walk in love, as Christ
also has loved us and given
Himself for us.*
Ephesians 5:2

CHAPTER 4

Move Over, Mother Teresa!

LANGUAGE 1: RESPONDERS

■

A *moan of deep pain. That is what it sounds like. Someone is in trouble. But where did the sound come from? There it is again. Over there in the ditch. Oh, no!* The man had been severely beaten and left for dead. He was in critical condition with open wounds and ugly bruises everywhere. *Uh-oh, he is a Jew. That does not matter; he needs help.*

Motivated by compassion and mercy, the good Samaritan reached out in love to remove his enemy's physical and emotional pain. Oblivious to his personal danger, and ignoring the age-old stigmas, he responded with his heart instead of his head. His empathy moved him to care tenderly for the cruelly treated stranger, even using his own supplies to bind the man's wounds and relieve his pain. Then going out of his way, he gently took the Jew on his own donkey to an inn to provide him comfort and ongoing care. He felt good about being able to help, gladly spending his own money to pay the man's bill. He was behaving in the compassionate language of a Responder, a language that Jesus knew and spoke fluently.

We have found from our research and testing that about one-third of the entire population have Responder as one of their top three languages. These people reach out to heal the wounds of a hurting world. Led by their feelings and emotions, Responders act from the sensitivity of the heart before they consult the intellect of the head.

To Responders, family is always important. They desire family harmony, sharing love, precious memories, photo albums, and the like. Responders who did not receive this as children crave family unity and involvement. In their jobs, they do not have coworkers; they adopt their coworkers as extended family members.

Responders say, "I feel," frequently, as compared to people who use the thinking (cognitive) languages and say, "I think," or the kinetic languages and "just do it" or say, "Do it."

Dr. David Swoap, in a commencement address at Westmont College, told the story of having met Mother Teresa once: "I asked her, 'Don't you ever become angry at the social injustice you see in India or other places you work?' Her gentle response was, 'Why should I expend energy in anger that I can expend in love?' "

That is truly the heart of a Responder. Love is the very core of the communication style.

Responders' Response to Life

Emotional heart decisions involving people and values indicate a feeling preference. Those who use their heads make a decision and then expect approval, but those who use their hearts prefer to get approval *before* making a decision.

Responders respond to life first with emotions. They feel, then act, then think.

Positive Characteristics of Responders

AFFECTIONATE

Responders are naturally affectionate and compassionate. They like to touch and hug. Their great empathy for others makes them deeply loyal friends and allows them to rejoice with those who are blessed and to grieve with those who are in pain. They feel whatever others around them are feeling, from exhilaration to depression.

CREATIVE

The emotive languages of Responder and Influencer tend to be creative in art, music, writing, dance, drama, or decorating.

SYMPATHETIC

With a great capacity to show love, Responders always look for good in people and situations. Their intense sympathy often draws them to people who are hurting or in distress, interceding in the hurts and problems of others. They are champions of underdogs.

JOYFUL

Responders are generally joyful and cheerful. These wonderful people often express and share their God-given joy through art, music, creative writing, dance, and/or drama, which they hope will help others find the same joy they have. They are imaginative and creative.

STRONG

Sometimes our society views the behavior of Responders as weak. Yet, the greatest strength of all is showing love and compassion and feeling deeply for others. Jesus was the most compassionate person who ever lived. As King of kings and Lord of lords, He knelt down in gentleness and compassion to heal sick people and comfort sorrowing people. His matchless power was displayed through His overwhelming mercy and kindness. Responders are merciful and kind, showing the Savior's love to people they meet.

LOVING

> **OF ALL THE SEVEN LANGUAGES, THIS ONE *SHOWS* THE MOST LOVE. PEOPLE WHO SPEAK THE OTHER LANGUAGES ACTUALLY LOVE JUST AS MUCH, BUT THE LANGUAGE OF RESPONDERS *SHOWS* IT THE MOST.**

Responders are happiest when they are giving and receiving love. They are huggers and hand holders.

NONCRITICAL

Responders are noncritical by nature. They consistently look for and see only the good in people. When negative characteristics are revealed about someone, Responders are always surprised. Because of this trait, they can be easily hurt, taken advantage of, or misunderstood.

SENSITIVE

Responders sense the hurt in others, respond to that hurt, and have a strong desire to make it go away. Of speakers of all the languages, these people are the most sensitive to the emotional status of others. They know if you are up or down, happy or sad, confident or fearful. Theirs is an intuitive discernment; they do not necessarily discern motives, just feelings. They are very sensitive to comprehending body language as well as hearing the emotional message or meaning behind someone's words. They tend to know if you mean something personally, or if you are disappointed in them; this is a sense or subconscious ability.

> **BECAUSE OF THEIR SENSITIVITY, RESPONDERS ATTRACT EVERYTHING FROM HURTING PEOPLE TO STRAY DOGS. TOTALLY FRIENDLESS BEINGS OF THE WORLD STAND IN LINE AT THEIR DOORS.**

We know a couple who own several rental cabins near a lake. They are constantly letting people with heartbreaking stories stay in the homes rent free. Both people are Responders. Their empathetic hearts rule their heads, and God continues to bless them.

TRUSTING

Responders seem to remain trusting, no matter how many times they get burned. They continue to expect the best of everyone. They continue to forgive and forget. Do they remind you of Jesus, the great Responder, who prayed for His murderers from the cross?

PEACEMAKERS

By nature, Responders avoid conflicts and confrontations at all costs. They like to build bridges between people, deploring broken relationships. Their fondest dream is to see the body of Christ and their families function in unity and love as God intended.

If children who are Responders live in a home where there is open conflict or fighting, they usually feel that it is their fault. They feel that if they were better children, their parents would not fight or get a divorce. The at-war atmosphere can seriously damage the emotional stability of the sensitive child who speaks the Responder language.

Desires of Responders

Responders have an overwhelming desire to comfort and ease the pain of others. Like the good Samaritan and Mother Teresa, they will go out of their way to help others. They willingly set themselves aside for the good of others. These are often the nurses and doctors of our world. These are the caregivers in hospices, retirement centers, children's homes, and physical therapy centers. These are the medical missionaries, the rescue teams that face treacherous terrain to save injured people, and the veterinarians who comfort defenseless animals.

Responders may also be authors who write self-help recovery books and sensitive poetry. They may be composers of such emotional music as "He Ain't Heavy, He's My Brother" or "Bridge Over Troubled Water." They may be the artists who paint the pain of Jesus on the cross, or an actor who portrays the compassion of Florence Nightingale.

Possible Negative Characteristics of Responders

The Responder can exhibit some negative or unhealthy traits when under stress, hurt, unhealthy, spiritually immature, or not being led by God's indwelling Spirit. Of all the seven languages, this one has the greatest capacity for good, but the wounded, abused, undernurtured, and underdeveloped Responder has the potential for alcoholism, drug abuse, eating disorders, suicide, and the need for psychiatric care.

> **IN A WAY, THIS LANGUAGE IS THE BEST AND THE WORST OF THEM ALL. IT CAN BE THE MOST SENSITIVE, COMPASSIONATE, AND GIVING, OR IT CAN BE THE MOST SELF-DESTRUCTIVE, UNHEALTHY, DEPENDENT ON OTHERS, AND EASILY SUBJECTED TO THE WRONG MASTER.**

Responders who are healthy can understand the heart of Christ and give unconditional love probably better than any other language.

DENIAL OF NEGATIVE EMOTIONS

Though ruled by their emotions, Responders have a difficult time owning and acknowledging their negative emotions. Rather than deal with bothersome feelings, they tend to stuff the negatives and deny them, hoping against hope that they will simply go away. They could appropriately wear the T-shirt we saw that read, "Cleopatra, Queen of Denial." Denial can be the source of many emotional, relational, and physical problems. The feelings that have been stuffed away often lead to depression and, eventually, addiction. Many people who are, in fact, Responders score low or even "0" on the Responder section of the quiz due to long-term denial.

TOLERANCE OF EVIL

Responders' fear of confrontation coupled with compassion may allow them to tolerate evil or wrongdoing. They cannot force themselves into a head-on battle or experience making someone feel bad. Their approach is to ignore the wrong and hope it will disappear on its own. You might say they suffer from the ostrich syndrome of sticking their heads in the sand. Obviously, that does not solve the problem; it is only a solution in the minds of Responders.

Result? Responders often end up with a pile of unresolved problems and dependent persons clinging to them, which again leaves them frustrated. For instance, they usually believe that with enough love, affection, and attention, a hurting person or angry mate or rebellious child will get better. So, instead of confronting the problem, they encourage the person, which many times only enables the person to continue the problem without feeling badly about it. Responders, in reality, can become a part of the problem, which is the last thing they want to do.

SCHEDULE SKIPPERS

Another possible negative trait of Responders is their here-and-now orientation. They are so distracted by what is in front of them right now that they have a hard time staying on schedule. They tend to be diddle-daddlers, taking care of insignificant details rather than concentrating on the significant project that is waiting.

For instance, a Responder will stop to water the houseplants she notices on the way out the door to an important meeting to which she is already late. The plants are here and now while the meeting is there and later. In reality, the plants would have been fine until she returned home after the meeting. Responders' lack of attention to time schedules often frustrates and irritates speakers of the more action-oriented languages to whom time is highly important. When Responders experience the frustration of the other speakers, they feel unloved, which is their greatest fear. Unfortunately, their bad feelings have often been self-inflicted.

Solution. Responders can learn to evaluate what they are doing based on real priorities by asking themselves questions. For instance, "Are these plants really more important to me than the children in my Sunday school class who are waiting for me?" Or "Is dusting this dresser really more important to me than my spouse, who is waiting for me in the car?" In reality, they are being controlled by their natural language of life, which is response to whatever they encounter. People who speak the other languages would tend to see this as indulging their feelings or as selfishness, but their actions do not really stem from a position of selfishness.

Responders can learn to think beyond their feelings by exercising their awareness of others' practical needs. For instance, they can develop the habit of asking themselves questions such as, "Are my time and feelings really more important than my spouse's time and feelings?" However, during times of stress or distress, they will probably revert to the former, more natural behavior.

EMPHASIS ON FEELINGS OVER FACTS

Doers, Strategists, Movers, and even Influencers are frustrated by Responders' heart-over-head approach to life. Responders do not analyze or rely on facts to make decisions. They determine their course of action based on feelings, which may be illogical at times. When the Spirit is not in control, these concepts can be both dangerous and ungodly.

If Responders do not feel like getting out of bed, they tend to sleep in, even when their actions affect someone else in a negative way. Or if they suddenly do not feel like going to a play, even though they have made plans with their mates or friends, they stay home, with little or no thought to how their last-minute change of plans may affect the other person. To Movers, Doers, and Strategists, this action is maddening, completely irresponsible, and totally selfish. Put a Responder and a Strategist in the same marriage, and look out! God may use them to bring balance to each other, but frustration will run high if they do not understand each other's behavioral language.

VULNERABILITY

> **BECAUSE THEY FEEL SO DEEPLY, RESPONDERS CAN ALSO BE HURT MORE DEEPLY. OF THE SPEAKERS OF ALL THE LANGUAGES, THEY ARE THE MOST VULNERABLE TO HURTS BECAUSE THEIR HEARTS ARE MOST OPEN TO OTHERS.**

When they are betrayed, there is virtually no tough hide or callousness to deflect the attack. It is then that these gentle people often develop various addictions to deal with their intense pain. They may turn to alcohol to drown their sorrows, begin taking drugs (legal or illegal) to restore their emotional highs, or turn to food and overeating as comfort.

MISUNDERSTOOD MOTIVES

Responders tend to be misunderstood. Being touchers, huggers, and more affectionate than most others, Responders' actions can be mistaken as sexual advances or signals. They need to guard against giving any "appearance of evil." They need to leave no room for misunderstandings or misinterpretations of their affections. They can do this by developing an awareness of how and when they hug, touch, and enter other people's personal space. They may need to deliberately distance themselves a bit from what feels spontaneously natural to them, recognizing other people's discomfort.

INDECISIVE

Not wanting to offend anyone for any reason, Responders tend to be indecisive. They do not want to upset someone by making the wrong decision. They would rather make no decision than the wrong one. They do not seem to understand that failure to make a decision *is* a decision. This trait may frustrate Movers, who make quick, usually accurate decisions and move on.

PAINFUL CHILDHOOD

Children who are Responders need the most protection, nurturing, and encouragement from their parents. If these needs are not met in childhood, in adulthood they will possibly need professional help to receive healing of their emotional hurts.

OWNERSHIP OF OTHERS' PROBLEMS

Responders tend to take up other people's offenses—they feel what you feel. This tendency sets the Responder up for more hurt. God gives grace for healing to the person who actually has the offense, but He may not give grace to a person who takes up someone else's offenses. Responders need to work at letting go of hurts—their own, both past and present, and those of others. If they are not mature in their emotions, they sympathize too much with other people rather than show helpful compassion and mercy.

> **SYMPATHY DOES NOT SET PEOPLE FREE. IT CAN, IN FACT, GIVE THEM COMFORT IN THEIR SELF-PITY AND PROLONG THE PROBLEM.**

UNFORGIVING

Responders hang on to their feelings. They tend to keep score of wrongs and hurts they experience. They may nurse a grudge to keep it alive for years just because they relish feelings—good or bad. As a result of their self-pity and pouting, Responders without the Spirit are usually slow to forgive. Meanwhile, that negative feeling eats away at the Responders' emotional health. If this is your language, please allow the Lord to heal you of your past hurts so that this beautiful language can develop into its fullest potential. Do not "quench the Spirit" in your life any longer.

FEAR OF CONFLICT

Responders are strongly influenced by their own and other people's needs and opinions. Operating in agreement with others and staying out of conflict are very important to them. They avoid conflict and confrontations because they dislike criticism. Carried to extreme, this tendency can be a weakness. Usually, Responders are tactful, diplomatic, and easily apologetic, hating to hurt the feelings of others. And although they hate conflict and disagreements, they are usually more often involved in them than speakers of the more cognitive languages because their sensitive emotions easily erupt over hurt feelings, rejections, and slights. Because they do not want to disappoint anyone, they many times say yes when they mean no.

Progressive Warning Signals of Distress

This predictive model indicates or predicts the sequence Responders go through in times of normal to severe stress.

Responders give off distress signals when they are under stress and have not gotten their batteries charged in positive ways. That is when unresolved issues from past hurts, toxic experiences, immaturity, and lack of reliance on the Holy Spirit emerge or reemerge. The length and depth of the problems, and their failure to deal with them, determine the degree of negative distress signals. When these distress signals appear, Responders sabotage their personal or professional lives in predictable ways:

- First-level distress warning signals. At this level, Responders overplease, try to keep "peace at all costs," and denigrate themselves, express low self-esteem, lose confidence, and pout.
- Second-level distress warning signals. Responders feel confused, make mistakes, feel "rattled," pout, withdraw, and get depressed. They move into denial and become defensive.
- Third-level distress warning signals. Finally, Responders act out self-doubt, feel rejected and unloved, sink further into depression, bitterness, blaming, and unforgiveness. They often seek relief through addictions and, in extreme cases, can be suicidal.

How Do I Love Thee?

AFFECTION AND UNCONDITIONAL ACCEPTANCE

Responders experience love when they are shown affection. They treasure personal contact, such as hugging, holding hands, and sitting close to you. Because they need to be listened to and allowed to share their feelings, Responders also want you to share your true feelings, even bad ones, with them. They want desperately to feel connected and in touch with you, both physically and emotionally. Responders require sensitivity and low conflict to thrive emotionally.

Mates need to allow Responders into our lives and personal space, sharing hugs and affection with them, because they will bring love and warmth to our lives. Men who are Responders love to open doors for women, and women who are Responders love for them to do it. They let people in front of them in the grocery line, theater ticket line, or traffic and feel good about it. They send cards and notes for all occasions and for no particular occasion, and they love to receive cards from us, especially sensitive and expressive ones. Usually, they keep the cards and read them again and again.

Because they are peaceable, Responders not only do not like confrontation but usually cannot handle it at all. They will do almost anything to avoid it, even to the detriment of their health. They may only hint at being unhappy about things, so mates of Responders need to be sensitive to these hints and deal with them gently and tenderly. If this is your language, ask God to show you how to be more honest, direct, and assertive about your feelings. Ask Him to help you overcome your fear of confrontation and openness.

To communicate with a Responder, do not expect the person to operate on your time schedule. Accepting this aspect without trying to change a Responder will lessen the frustration and constant confrontation for both of you.

SPIRITUAL MOTIVATION

Each of the seven behavioral languages correlates to one of the motivational gifts listed in Romans 12:5–8. The Responder's behavioral style generally correlates to the motivational gift of mercy. Each gift of grace is vital to the health and growth of the church, the body of Christ. The Responder role models the gift of mercy and teaches us to love one another deeply, with compassion and gentleness.

FINANCIAL STYLE

Responders are generally not too logical or methodical in the financial arena. They can live within a budget—but with difficulty.

They tend to make decisions based on how they feel at the moment, which can lead to spontaneous spending. It can also lead to buyer's remorse later when they get home with something and wonder why they bought it. Responders may spend a lot of their time returning items. One thing in their favor of not spending foolishly is that they do not make decisions too quickly; they may delay following their feelings when purchasing is a temptation.

ENTERTAINMENT STYLE

Responders always seem to have lots of friends. Probably their most popular entertainment style is having friends drop in because they know they are always welcome, whether in the morning for coffee, in the evening, or on weekends. Responders tend to make others feel welcome anytime, and they are never too busy to stop what they are doing and listen to others.

When they formally entertain, Responders can be comfortable with all sizes of groups, but they generally prefer smaller groups so that they can really get to know each other or share with each other. Their dinner parties or events may have many things left to do at the last minute because they do not get around to doing the practical things ahead of time. Responders generally are not bothered by these unfinished things, and they joyfully allow others to pitch in and help. In fact, as soon as help arrives, Responders may wander into the living room to visit while their friends complete the practical tasks.

THE HOME

The feeling or atmosphere of the home is of utmost importance to Responders. They are not as concerned about the functional aspects of the home as the way the home feels to them aesthetically. They want their homes to be reflections of the love and warmth of the family, homes that give a sense of security and safety, that provide protection from the outside world and all its unknown, perceived dangers. Their homes tend to be nestlike and symbolically nurturing. They will be filled with family photos, mementos from family vacations and trips, and other sentimental objects. They like their homes to be lovely to look at, filled with fresh flowers and beautiful music. As a matter of fact, pleasing art, beautiful flowers, a glorious view, and music actually energize or charge the battery of Responders. They get depressed or distressed without sensory nurturing. Most Responders like their homes to be somewhat open to light because they tend to feel depressed in dark areas. They like bright, inviting colors used in the decor and an open, airy, lots-of-plants feeling.

RESPONDERS AND SEX

Of the speakers of all the languages, Responders, both the men and the women, tend to be the most sensitive lovers. They want their mates to share their feelings and listen to them with emotional understanding throughout the day in order for them to be emotionally prepared for intimate sexual moments. Romantic atmospheres with music, soft lights, planned evenings, and lots of reassurance, holding, and cuddling are vital to meaningful intimate moments with mates.

Responders have difficulty being intimate and romantic when they do not feel like it. It is hard for them to learn that they can make a decision to be sexually intimate, even if they are tired or not in a good mood. Sexual communication, like verbal communication, takes commitment and conscious decision. Responders, both men and women, like to be held sometimes rather than being sexually intimate.

Because they respond to people and life with strong emotions, Responders can sometimes be sexually tempted. They are usually responding to persons who need love or understanding. The emotional attraction is Responders' desire to meet other people's needs, not necessarily a sexual attraction. However, before they know it, they can find themselves in a compromising situation. Responders need predetermined guidelines that are safety nets for themselves.

For instance, we have a Responder friend who is a businessman. A personal guideline is that he will never close the door to his office when his secretary is in the room with him. He never takes his secretary to lunch alone, even if it is Secretaries' Day or her birthday. Through the years, he has had some secretaries who were young and some who were old enough to be his mother, but he treated them all the same. He is a wise man because he knows that he is vulnerable to emotional situations, and he does not want to take any chances with his spiritual life.

Responders so naturally demonstrate their affection freely that they can be misunderstood by the opposite sex. Their hugs can be seen as come-ons, and their touching can be considered sexual advances. Though Responders may mean no such thing, people of other behavioral styles may be misled by Responders' reach-out-and-touch-someone approach to life. So, Responders often need to take one step back from their natural tendency to avoid leaving wrong impressions.

Candid Camera

An interesting combination of languages occurs when a Responder is married to an Influencer.

We were conducting a language seminar in Ohio and asked each person to take the "Language Discovery Quiz." That was on a Friday night, and we were to resume the seminar the next morning at nine. We had a phone call in our room at 7:00 A.M. from an excited couple who asked to meet us for breakfast. Over ham and eggs we listened to this precious couple share how they had been up almost all night discussing the test results, laughing, crying, hugging, asking forgiveness, and forgiving.

They were one of many couples who come to our seminars almost as a last-ditch hope for a miracle. Many couples have attended who were separated and had already filed for divorce, and caring friends would bring them separately to the seminar. We have seen God work wonders as He restores hope and marriages.

This couple, Tim and Terry, were not separated physically, but they were separated emotionally and spiritually. They had separated themselves from each other to avoid further hurt, frustration, and anger. Since both of their languages were emotive, both were easily hurt or wounded.

Tim, a Responder, was greatly distressed by their marriage conflicts. Responders do not handle an environment of high conflict well. He felt that he had tried and tried to please Terry, but she did not respond. So, he began to internalize rejection, which led to depression, bitterness, and unforgiveness—all affecting his performance at work. He had seen his doctor about taking medication for depression. Tim felt that his marriage had become so destructive that to succeed in life, he had to build a wall between himself and Terry just to survive. Fortunately, they did not yet have any children because a cold war was in progress in their home.

Terry, an Influencer, was reacting to stressful issues by attempting to control Tim through overtalking and blaming him for her feelings. She was also moving into the second- and third-level distress warning signals by feeling rejected, depressed, and trapped. She felt as if there was no way out of a hopeless, painful marriage. While Tim was building a wall between them to try to have a safe place to survive, Terry was just as busy trying to build an escape route out of the pain.

They saw themselves so clearly in that seminar. They reacted with jubilation and amazement. They felt that we had followed them home and taped their interaction as if on "Candid Camera." But they were excited by seeing the strength of both languages. They now loved the strengths they saw in each other and were inspired by the hope that things could get better. We spent time with them before the next session but had to leave right after the seminar. However, they stayed in touch with us, we had follow-up counseling via telephone, and about four months after we first met them, they flew to Dallas and spent a weekend with us to work on specific issues.

Terry and Tim have so much in common, it would be a shame for them not to make a good marriage. Yet they also share many negatives that can easily cause them to repel each other. Both are caring, loving, responsive, and affectionate, and they have the needed qualities to make the marriage work. One of their most important areas of compatibility is their love of the Lord. They desire to please Him, and they want their marriage to be a testimony of His faithfulness in their lives. They discovered the verse in Malachi where God says He hates divorce (2:16), and they made a renewed commitment to each other that they would not again entertain the idea of divorce, nor would they (when they were in the heat of emotions) threaten each other with divorce. These decisions, based on their convictions, are now stronger than their feelings, and they are seeing marriage as a process of learning to live and love in a healthy, constructive relationship.

A Final Word with Feeling

A little girl was sent on an errand by her mother. She took much too long in coming back home, and her mother asked for an explanation. The little girl explained that on her way home she had met a friend who was crying because she had broken her doll.

"Oh," said the mother, "then you stopped to help her fix her doll?"

"No," said the little girl, "I stopped to help her cry."

That is the language of Responders, tenderly sharing in the hurts and joys of others. They want to feel with you and you with them. That's all.

> **MARRIAGE IS LIKE TWIRLING A BATON, TURNING HANDSPRINGS, OR EATING WITH CHOPSTICKS. IT LOOKS EASY UNTIL YOU TRY IT.**
> **—HELEN ROWLAND**

Influencer

Creative

Optimistic

Relational

*For we cannot but speak the
things which we have
seen and heard.*
Acts 4:20

CHAPTER 5

Life's Cheerleaders

LANGUAGE 2: INFLUENCERS

■

I t was a dark and stormy night . . . really! I (Fred) was teaching a Bible study at a friend's house. Anna was at our home in Dallas with our college-age son, Michael, and one of Michael's friends. Anna was listening to whistling winds and watching the churning inky skies out the patio door when suddenly a flash of lightning helped her see a deadly black tornado whirling straight toward our house. Anna flung open the patio door as she yelled for everyone to get into the bathroom. Then she dashed to open the front door. Michael immediately came along behind her and closed both doors, screaming that he had read you should not open the doors after all.

Anna, Michael's friend, and our two dogs dashed into the bathroom, and all of them took what cover they could in the bathtub. But Michael was missing! Anna shouted for him, then ran out into the hall. Michael was trying to pull his mattress down the hall to cover them for protection, but it was stuck in the doorway to the bedroom. Finally, abandoning the mattress, he and Anna jumped into the tub with the others.

Seconds later the storm hit full force. The roaring winds caused the pipes in the house to wheeze and hum, accompanied by the sounds of our roof being ripped off by the devastating tornado. The splintering, crashing noises included the demolition of the roof over our den, master bedroom, and garage. A large tree was uprooted and hurled through the window of Anna's car that was in the driveway, while electrical lines were yanked loose, plunging the house into the terror of uncertain blackness.

In the midst of all this panic, Anna was quoting every Scripture she could think of one after the other at the top of her voice, the dogs were howling and barking frantically, Michael was calling on God to still the storm in the name of Jesus, and Michael's friend was crying hysterically.

The departing tornado was followed by eerie calm and complete silence, like the heavy silence of a tomb long since sealed. Providentially, no one was hurt.

Finally, Michael said, "Mom, I think it's over."

"No, we have to wait," said Anna. "Remember, we are in the eye of the storm. We have to wait until the rest of the storm comes through."

"Mom, we're not on the coast now; this is Dallas. A hurricane has an eye, not a tornado."

"Oh, yeah," laughed Anna nervously. "I forgot."

The electricity was off, but the phone was still working. Anna called me immediately at the Bible study to tell me what had happened while Michael looked for a flashlight or candles.

Now, time out for a minute. You must understand at this point that Influencers like Anna, in their excitement to tell the best story they can, have a tendency to exaggerate reality a bit. I can remember Anna's calling me at my office one time to tell me that our Christian bookstore had flooded and was "two feet deep in water." When I got there, after breaking all the speed laws in town, it was more like an inch deep in water. There are other such "wolf" stories I could tell you as well, but I will forgo them for now. Keep that in mind, though.

When Anna told me that the roof was off the house, I naturally reacted with less panic than she expected. As I was rushing home (just in case she was not exaggerating this time), I was praying fervently that she was truly exhibiting the normal trait of an Influencer to enhance the telling of exciting news. For once I was disappointed to find that no enhancement was needed; the reality was far more dramatic than Anna could have ever been.

Torrential rain continued for the next several days. We constructed a temporary roof, but with the ongoing heavy rains, we had a nightmarish surprise on the third night. The ceiling in the master bedroom had absorbed so much water that it collapsed onto our bed about three o'clock in the morning. Michael heard the crash and came running into our room. There we stood in the middle of the bed covered with black, wet globs of insulation.

Michael and I did not say a word. We rushed to the garage and got shovels, brooms, mops, and garbage bags. When we got back into the bedroom, Anna was still standing there in the middle of the bed soaking wet, red hair plastered against her face, hands set defiantly on her hips, and fighting back tears. In the typical optimistic style of an Influencer, she declared in the style of Scarlett in *Gone with the Wind*, "I don't care what happens. We're not going to let this stupid storm steal our joy or rob us of our faith!"

With that dramatic proclamation we all three fell into a heap on the slippery floor and broke into gales of laughter. The laughing was a good stress release, much better than screaming and yelling, which at that point were our only other alternatives. Then we looked around our storm-struck house, we talked about what we had to be thankful for, and in the midst of the disaster we rejoiced. Once again, as is often the case, Anna's ability to verbalize her optimism and enthusiasm for life brought us through the storm and back into the calm.

Peter the Influencer

The apostle Peter was probably an Influencer like Anna. He often spoke without thinking. He was naturally impulsive (see Matt. 14:28; 17:4; John 21:7). Yet, he became the leader and spokesman of Jesus' chosen twelve world evangelists.

Peter's leadership abilities were tied to his strong beliefs, his excitement for the Lord, and his ability to communicate, inspire, and motivate other people. He was persuasive and able to articulate the vision of Christ for saving the world in a way that others could glimpse the dream and want to chase it. Even after Pentecost, Peter remained excited and focused on the power and teaching of Jesus.

No doubt, and according to familiar stories in the Bible, Peter was far from perfect. His obvious faults and weaknesses consistently got him into trouble with other people, but he was still one of the three privileged witnesses to such intimate and significant events as the Transfiguration and the Lord's agony in the Garden of Gethsemane. Later, Peter became a miracle worker and a powerful proclaimer of the saving message of Christ (see the book of Acts for examples).

Like other Influencers, Simon (as Peter was named originally) was impetuous and sometimes undependable. Jesus saw great potential in Simon, though, and changed his name to Peter, which means "the rock," a strong and dependable leader. And eventually, Peter became the person Jesus envisioned him to be.

Like Peter, Influencers can become strong and dependable leaders when they use their natural abilities and gifts according to God's plan for them. The first step is to recognize and understand these natural traits and abilities.

Influencers' Response to Life

Influencers react with feeling, then by thinking, and finally by acting. Usually, the feeling and the thinking are very close together. They automatically, and almost simultaneously, access their feelings and their thinking. Then there is usually a pause or waiting period while they talk about it, to others or to themselves through self-talk, before they go into action.

Positive Characteristics of Influencers

ORGANIZING, EDITING, AND SPEAKING AT ONCE

Influencers usually organize, edit, and speak their ideas as they are talking. Because they are quite skilled at communicating and are mentally agile, they pull this off fairly well. Many times Influencers do not know what they are going to say until after it is said. Garrison Keillor, author and radio personality of "Prairie Home Companion," a syndicated program from Minnesota Public Radio, said, "I talk and talk until I think of something to say." Influencers readily voice their opinions, volunteering how they feel, what they think, how much something costs, and what they are doing. Many times Influencers are attracted to the people who speak less verbal languages because they are such good listeners.

OPTIMISTIC

INFLUENCERS ARE POSITIVE AND ENCOURAGING, THE NATURAL CHEERLEADERS IN LIFE.

They truly believe in people and are eager to tell them "you can do it," "you can make it," "keep trying; you will overcome." They look for positive life examples and are motivated by positive feelings, thoughts, and actions. Even when things go wrong or there is a problem, trial, crisis, or disaster, they can be optimistic because they believe that "this, too, shall pass," and things will get better. When they are down or discouraged, it is usually only a short time until Influencers are back up, feeling good about life again.

> **THEY ARE THE PERSUADERS, MOTIVATORS, AND ENCOURAGERS OF THE REST OF US.**

FORWARD THINKERS

Influencers generally are not status quo people, nor do they tend to cling to the past. They could be described as forward-thinking people, looking forward to the next project, new ideas, discoveries, and adventures. Like the apostle Paul, they forget the past and press on toward their goals.

RELATIONSHIP ORIENTED

People are of primary significance to Influencers. Relationships are much more important than things, accomplishments, or tasks. They are highly sociable, and they need interactive relationships and good communication. Relationships energize them; they are people people. An Influencer's theme might be "People who need people are the luckiest people in the world."

GROWTH VALUED

An example of Influencers' discontent with status quo is their desire for personal growth, both for themselves and for others. Change is not frightening to them; they see it as necessary to growth. They try new ideas, projects, and methods and encourage others to do so.

> **INFLUENCERS ARE LEARNERS AND SEEKERS; THEY NEVER RETIRE FROM THE SEARCH FOR KNOWLEDGE AND EXPERIENCES THAT EXPAND THEIR PARADIGMS.**

PERCEPTION OF SOLUTIONS

They view growth for themselves or others as being achieved through positive solutions, which seem automatic to them. They quite naturally verbalize the necessary steps required to produce growth, change, improvement, or recovery. You may often hear an Influencer saying, "The first thing we need to do is . . . , then we can do this." They are solution oriented, automatically looking for solutions to problems.

COMMUNICATORS

Influencers are comfortable expressing their thoughts, feelings, dreams, visions, ideas, love, care, and appreciation. They can be articulate, exciting, and persuasive. Because communication is easy for them, most other people are comfortable with them, and they can draw other people into conversations. Communicating is essential to Influencers, and that communication involves more than words; it requires understanding and being understood. It is their way of reaching out and making connections with other people.

ACCEPTING

Usually not judgmental toward others, Influencers tend to accept others where they are, with what they have done or been, and love them as they are. This acceptance is not a blindness that the person is perfect. On the contrary, they basically see everyone as imperfect; to them, no one has really arrived, and yet no one is a complete failure. We are all in the process of becoming. They expect people to have problems and struggles, including themselves; it is part of the growth process of human beings.

EASE OF DECISIONS

Influencers tend to make decisions easily and quickly. They do not usually take themselves or life too seriously, and they feel that if the decision is wrong, God will help them correct it. This ease in decision making is also tied to their positive, optimistic attitude toward life, and their desire to embrace life and get on with living. They do not want to waste time being undecided or dillydallying. Theirs is a "go for it" attitude that usually pays off.

MANY FRIENDS

Because Influencers are positive cheerleaders, they are fun to be around, and people tend to gravitate toward them. They are often the ones elected as "best liked," "most likely to succeed," king or queen of something, or class president in high school and college. They radiate with joy, life, and excitement.

DIPLOMATIC AND TACTFUL

Influencers are among the most diplomatic speakers of the behavioral languages. Even though they do not always edit their words, they are natural people pleasers. They believe in people, and they desire to build others up. Even when they have to criticize someone, Influencers do not like to hurt anyone's feelings, so they are positive, uplifting, and tactful in pointing out problem areas.

FUN-LOVING AND GOOD SENSE OF HUMOR

Influencers enjoy life. They find humor and joy in life's situations without carrying the troubles of the world around with them. They tend to play first; then they are energized to work. Playing energizes their creativity, and they demonstrate to others how to have fun. Influencers may have some difficulty in school, not because of intelligence (this is not an IQ issue) but because schools are usually taught by and to the more cognitive learners, geared to the more cognitive languages. Influencers like to have fun. If they are allowed to do this, especially in elementary school, they will be energized to move into their cognitive abilities.

LEARNING BY DOING

Influencers like to try it—whatever it is. They are the first to jump into the ocean without even testing the water's temperature. The world presents itself to Influencers and they jump on. They want to experience life for themselves, and they show their friends and families new aspects of life. They learn by doing whatever they find to do.

METICULOUS OR CREATIVE APPEARANCE

Influencers seem to want to look their best, put their best foot forward, and make good impressions. So, they are concerned about their personal appearance and the look of their homes, offices, or other environments.

FEEDBACK NEEDED

Influencers need to know that they are constantly connecting with someone. In conversations, they need for you to nod your head or give a verbal acknowledgment that you are hearing them, such as these: "Yes"; "I understand"; "Uh-huh"; "wow"; "I see." When people give no visible feedback, Influencers get frustrated and confused.

LISTENING VALIDATION REQUIRED

Because Influencers think while talking, talking is their way of thinking through something. If mates think this is a call to action or a need for advice, they will be mistaken. Influencers just need someone to listen, validate them, and perhaps mirror back to them what they said. Once this happens, they are generally good at analyzing their situations and coming to accurate conclusions. They also are usually open to asking for advice or help when it is needed.

INCLUSIVE

Though speakers of some languages tend to segregate or compartmentalize their relationships, Influencers like to include, introduce, and connect theirs. If they like someone, they want to introduce that person to everyone else they like. Because of this, whether socially or professionally,

> **THEY ARE GOOD NETWORKERS. IF YOU WANT TO GET TO KNOW KEY PEOPLE IN MANY AREAS OF LIFE, GET TO KNOW INFLUENCERS, AND THEY WILL HELP YOU MEET THE REST.**

CREATIVE

Influencers usually have a flair for the creative somewhere in their makeup, whether it is in music, the arts, sewing, decorating, drama, dance, writing, crafts, or public speaking. You will likely see the flamboyant or creative expressed in various aspects of their lives.

Desires of Influencers

Influencers desire to meet the psychological-relationship needs of others. They want healthy relationships, and they want others to have healthy relationships. They desire to build people up so that they can reach their full potential. They believe that to live victoriously, we must have healthy relationships with God and others, and their greatest desire is to help people achieve them.

While both Responders and Influencers are concerned about the emotional-psychological needs of others, Responders will be sympathetic, compassionate, and comforting to another who is in pain, usually for as long as that person hurts. They continue to be sympathetic and do not try to change the other person.

Influencers are concerned about others' emotional pain and health and want them to live victorious, healthy, and growing lives. Influencers will be empathetic to someone who is in pain; then they will encourage and challenge the person to move out of the pain and into solutions that will lead to victory. They encourage change and growth. However, if someone wants to stay in his or her pain or problem and not grow or overcome, Influencers will not show ongoing patience as the Responder does.

Possible Negative Characteristics of Influencers

NEGATIVE CONVERSATIONAL HABITS

Talking without thinking and being uncomfortable with silence cause Influencers to be guilty of talking too much and too often. Influencers can easily do most of the talking and not allow others to participate, which can be their way of controlling others and situations. When there is a lull in the conversation, and even when silence is appropriate, Influencers will try to fill it with words, even if they do not make sense. They have to learn to accept and appreciate silence. Influencers may walk into a room talking, causing disruption to another conversation already going on, without being aware that they are causing others to be annoyed.

TENDENCY TO INTERRUPT OTHERS OR FINISH SENTENCES FOR THEM

Influencers are so excited about communication that they generally do not realize that they interrupt others. When confronted about this issue, they are usually surprised. When their mates complain that they finish their sentences for them, they are genuinely surprised that this bothers their mates because they are just joining in, showing interest, or adding to what is being said. This tendency may also cause them to be poor listeners.

SEEMINGLY CRITICAL

Influencers are not really critical. As a matter of fact, they are among the most accepting speakers of all the languages. Two of their positive qualities actually combine to make them seem critical: (1) they are accepting of people where they are, but they do not want to see them stay there, and (2) they desire for all to grow, change, and become everything God created them to be. This exuberant desire for victorious growth may come across too strongly or intensely and make others feel that they are being judged because they do not measure up.

IMPATIENT

Influencers are impatient with people who are not solution oriented but want to remain in their problems, who are complaining, or who exhibit self-pity. This impatience may come across as a lack of compassion. But Influencers have great patience with and compassion for people who *are* seeking solutions to life's problems and will always be there to cheer them on.

POLLYANNAISH ATTITUDE

People may view Influencers as unrealistic because of their overly positive attitude. Others may think that Influencers do not operate in reality. They do; it is just that their reality may be more optimistic than that of people with other behavioral characteristics.

NOT IN-DEPTH STUDENTS

Influencers have quick minds and can get by on a few good buzzwords; therefore, they may tend to operate on surface knowledge rather than with all of the facts. They seem well informed on a large variety of subjects, but sometimes their reliance on insufficient information catches up with them.

INVOLVEMENT IN MORE PROJECTS THAN THEY CAN FINISH

Influencers are interested in many things, and they like to be involved in many things, so they often start more than they can finish. However, because they usually work well under pressure, they usually get the important things done.

DIFFICULTY WITH OWNING NEGATIVE FEELINGS

Influencers are good persuaders and can convince themselves that they are not hurt, angry, or disappointed. They can be in denial a lot as a result. Although expressing their positive and happy feelings comes as easily as breathing, they usually have to learn to recognize their negative side, stop stuffing their negative feelings, and learn healthy ways of dealing with them.

MANIPULATORS

Most Influencers do not have to learn to manipulate themselves and others; it comes naturally. They have to learn to recognize that they do it and may need help in overcoming the tendency. They can usually get by with being manipulative because they are tactful, charming, and persuasive. They slide over into manipulation without even knowing it. However, being manipulative can be destructive to their integrity and their spiritual and emotional relationships. People close to them may build up resentment and start feeling used by Influencers. They may manipulate others in the name of delegating, but it is really manipulating.

EXAGGERATION

Influencers are generally good storytellers, love to communicate, and want their conversations to be interesting and hold the audience's attention. So, exaggerating becomes second nature if that is what it takes. Influencers must allow the Lord to control their speech. When Influencers become Christians, the Lord brings conviction of honesty and truthfulness into their lives.

ALL TALK AND NO ACTION

True to their nature, Influencers love to sit and talk. They can talk for hours, seldom noticing the mundane things around them that call for their attention. This can be frustrating to mates who speak kinetic languages, such as Doers and Movers.

FORMULA FOLLOWERS

To Influencers, solutions may become so cut and dried that they are like formulas. Unfortunately (or perhaps fortunately), the principles of God and life cannot be reduced to rigid formulas.

TENDENCY TO BECOME VERBALLY ABUSIVE

If Influencers operate from these negative characteristics rather than the positive ones listed earlier, and if they are not close to the Lord, they can become verbally abusive. This abuse may take the form of name-calling, haranguing someone, or being obsessed with a subject and not letting up.

Progressive Warning Signals of Distress

This predictive model indicates or predicts the sequence Influencers go through in times of normal to severe stress.

Influencers signal their distress in several ways when they have not gotten their batteries charged in positive ways. Distress may cause unresolved issues to emerge and reemerge. These issues come from past hurts, toxic experiences, immaturity, stress, and lack of reliance on the Holy Spirit. The length and depth of the problems, and their failure to deal with them, determine the degree of negative distress signals. When these distress signals appear, Influencers dysfunction and sabotage their personal or professional lives in predictable ways:

- First-level distress warning signals. At this level, Influencers exhibit exaggeration, manipulation, and control of others through talking too much or overselling themselves and their thoughts and feelings.
- Second-level distress warning signals. When Influencers move on to this level of distress, they add to the first level by denying their feelings of responsibility in a matter, blaming others, and overemphasizing formulas for answers.

- Third-level distress warning signals. They finally feel rejected and may move into destructive behavior, such as depression, feeling trapped and wanting to run away, or an attitude that says, "I'll show you," "I don't need you," "I'll reject you before you reject me." Schoolchildren who do not get the positive attention and reinforcement they need from their parents may act out to get negative attention. To them, even negative attention is better than no attention. Influencers often become verbally abusive in unchecked third-level distress.

How Do I Love Thee?

AFFIRMATION

> **INFLUENCERS NEED AFFIRMATION AND ENCOURAGEMENT FROM THEIR MATES. THEY FEEL LOVED WHEN THEY ARE TOLD THAT THEY ARE LOVED.**

Although they like affectionate hugs, special moments, gifts, and nice things done for them, these wonderful things are not as important to them as hearing "I love you," "you're wonderful," "I'm thankful for you," "you did a good job," and the like. They need affirmations, encouraging words, and expressions of love.

> **WHETHER IN PERSON, ON THE PHONE, OR BY MAIL, WORDS OF LOVE MAKE THEM FEEL SECURE.**

Influencers feel loved when you allow them to express their thoughts, feelings, and dreams while you carefully listen and affirm them. Your allowing them to use their God-appointed language of verbal expression endears you to them. Influencers also need for you to tell them your thoughts and feelings. They need your personal contact and verbal interaction. Influencers have a vital need to experience playful contact with you, which in turn energizes their serious side.

SPIRITUAL MOTIVATION

Each of the seven behavioral languages correlates to one of the motivational gifts listed in Romans 12:5–8. The Influencer's behavioral style generally correlates to the spiritual gift of exhortation. Each gift of grace is vital to the health and growth of the church, the body of Christ. Influencers encourage us to be our best for the Lord.

FINANCIAL STYLE

Because they are spur-of-the-moment, spontaneous people, Influencers tend to carry this style into their buying or spending practices. However, due to their creativity, they may find ways to build a secure financial base, but usually it is not so much from a practical desire to save money as it is for a creative outlet that may be channeled toward finances. When they shop, they expect high levels of attention and like good quality.

Since they move rather rapidly from their feelings to their logic (thinking), they can be good money managers. They are not excited about the day-to-day management of money, but when the responsibility is theirs, they are capable of doing a thorough job of it. Since they operate in steps of action and formulas, they can be quite effective once they formalize money management. They tend to handle it in a short-range way, though, not on a five-year plan.

ENTERTAINMENT STYLE

Gregarious Influencers enjoy a great variety of people. They like small groups, large groups, and one-on-one situations. They just like people. They are happy entertaining—from convention-size masses to a quiet evening talking to one friend over coffee into the wee hours of the morning. Other people energize them. They are comfortable with planned, organized entertainment, but they also enjoy spontaneous events. They will drop what they are doing on the spur of the moment to entertain or participate in someone else's spontaneous activity. They seem to really like shows, plays, music, and the like where there are creativity and entertainment.

THE HOME

Influencers generally do not think of the practical or functional aspects of a home. They like creative, artistic, or dramatic effects. Rooms, furniture, bookshelves, and kitchens are arranged according to the feeling and the aesthetic appeal, not the function. The way a home feels, both inside and out, is very important to them. They usually want to achieve a definite feeling in their homes. Whether the home is open or cozy, down a tree-shaded lane or up on a high hill, they usually have a feeling that they look for more than a style.

Their homes' appearance is very important to them. They want their homes to be attractive and inviting to friends and family. There will be pictures of friends and family throughout their homes.

Their offices and homes are usually full of stimulation. They like both sound and visual stimulation. They like music, entertainment, TVs, and VCRs, and they may have gadgets on their desks. They love to live or work in a colorful location with a beautiful view, and they probably change their pictures and decor often. Lovely artwork and music throughout the home and a pleasing view are all important to them.

INFLUENCERS AND SEX

Because this is an emotive language, Influencers' feelings need to be activated for meaningful sexual activities. They like to hear words of love and affirmation, and they need to feel connected emotionally during sexual interplay with their mates. Both men and women Influencers respond well to being held, cuddled, and talked to affirmingly and affectionately.

Because of Influencers' need to talk, to understand, and to be understood, they usually talk (or can learn to talk) about sex, and they can be comfortably open about the subject.

Influencers must guard their hearts with genuine love and respect of the Lord, hate evil, and flee sexual temptation. Because the emotions are activated first, speakers of this emotive language can respond inappropriately to sexual temptation, thinking it is just a game and that they can handle it. They may find out too late that they are too close to the edge. Influencers must operate in the reality that the only safe way to handle temptation is to flee. The fact that they feel and then immediately think can be their saving grace because once they check their reasoning and logic, they will usually come back to the safety of their convictions.

A Hopeless Marriage

Jim and Maurine came to us for counseling. Jim could not believe that, after twenty-three years of marriage and being in the ministry together, Maurine wanted a divorce. Jim was an Influencer; Maurine was a Contemplator.

Maurine's story was that she listened to Jim talk all the way to church, then she listened to him preach, and after church, he talked about himself, the Lord, and the church. All the way home he would talk about the same things, and this pattern went on all day long, seven days a week.

Jim told Maurine what she was feeling, thinking, and planning. Maurine liked to think about things, think before she spoke, and think before she acted. As she would pause to think, Jim would take off. He thought her hesitation was his license to jump in and talk. He would interrupt her, finish her sentences, and not listen to her. He manipulated her by not giving her direct requests when asking her to do something for him. That sounds like a little thing until your day is filled with constant statements that make you feel used and manipulated, you are devalued by being interrupted and not listened to, and you are not allowed to have your own thoughts and feelings. One day Maurine started crying, withdrew, and would not make contact with Jim at all. She seemed to totally withdraw into her own little world and stayed that way for days. When she finally came out of her isolation, she said she never wanted to see or talk to Jim again.

After two counseling sessions, Jim was asked to review what had happened in the last two sessions. He could remember only what he had said, not what Maurine had had an opportunity to say or what the counselor had said. He also remembered what he did not get to say, even though he had done most of the talking.

Jim was raised in a home with very little healthy positive reinforcement or emotional bonding. He spent most of his time moving up and down the three levels of distress signals. There were intervals when he operated from his language strengths, and those were the times when he was successful, when people loved him, when he was open, honest, and transparent with Maurine. Unfortunately, he operated most of the time as a toxic Influencer, causing his relationships with his wife and children to be unhealthy and destructive, especially when he would hit third-level distress and become verbally abusive. Jim had no idea what they were upset about or what he had done wrong because he spent much of his time in second-level distress, denying feelings and responsibility and blaming others.

The good news is that Jim and Maurine received counseling, things improved, and they now understand the importance of working on their individual issues. They have a lifetime to share, and it will always take effort for Jim to see that he is doing anything wrong and to listen more and talk less. Maurine is learning to stand up for her rights, and instead of keeping everything inside until she withdraws from Jim, the children, and the world, she stops Jim, tells him she wants to talk, and asks him to please listen. She is learning to express her thoughts, feelings, and desires, and although it is still not easy for him, Jim is learning to stop, look, and listen to his wife, or to be with her in silence. He is learning that this is his way of honoring her and showing his love. Both are becoming sensitive when either of them moves into distress signals, and they are realizing that they can make a choice to be healthy, supportive, and loving.

Hip, Hip, Hooray!

God's cheerleaders, Influencers, are vital to speakers of all the other languages of love. They encourage us to be the very best we can be, using our own abilities and talents. They accept us as we are and bring spontaneity and joy to our lives. First Corinthians 8:1 describes Influencers very well: "Love . . . edifies and builds up and encourages one [to grow to his full stature]" (AMPLIFIED).

A HAPPY MARRIAGE IS A LONG CONVERSATION THAT SEEMS ALL TOO SHORT.
—ANDRÉ MAUROIS

Cognitive Languages
The Thinkers

- ## The Strategist
  ### Proverbs 16:9

- ## The Contemplator
  ### Proverbs 23:7

- ## The Giver
  ### 2 Corinthians 9:7

People who speak cognitive languages generally respond to life, people, and values first with their heads, then with their hearts and actions.

The cognitive languages are the behavioral styles that begin in the mind. They are the intellectual languages, the mentally active languages. Speakers of these languages think first, then they either feel or act. Their way of handling life's decisions is through thinking, reasoning, and deliberating—the intellectual exercises of activating their cognitive processes.

Probably the character who represents the pure cognitive personality to an entire generation of TV watchers is Mr. Spock, science officer on the original "Star Trek" series. Mr. Spock was cool, calculating, totally logical, nonemotional, all-knowing, nonfeeling, humorless, and lacking in many of our more important human qualities. Spock was loved and admired by Captain Kirk, probably a Strategist, but he was annoying and frustrating to Dr. McCoy (a Responder, no doubt).

Fortunately, people who speak the cognitive languages—Strategists, Contemplators, and Givers—have more endearing human qualities than Mr. Spock and are more balanced in their approaches to life. Still, each of them will have some of his cognitive characteristics.

Strategist

Organized

Visionary

Focused

The human mind plans the way,
but the LORD directs the steps.
Proverbs 16:9 NRSV

CHAPTER 6

Leading the Charge!

LANGUAGE 3: STRATEGISTS

■

W ar!" The giant headline screamed out at us from the front page of every newspaper in the United States. Our nation came to a virtual standstill as we became petrified spectators, sitting as stone statues in front of our television sets for hours every day, watching the play-by-play action of Operation Desert Storm. Tanks, jeeps, infantry, missiles, helicopters, and bombers were all in hot pursuit of Sadam Hussein and his Iraqi military.

Then a great Strategist stepped onto the Middle Eastern battle-field, and the war took a distinct turn. Do you remember when General H. Norman Schwarzkopf held his first press conference and described in great detail the step-by-step opening moves of the war? He used graphs, charts, maps, and diagrams of how troops from allied countries moved here, circled around there, and attacked from above. He was organized and confident, the obvious supreme leader of Operation Desert Storm. His strategic military genius made him an instant hero to Americans, an honor he will no doubt wear throughout history, like his Strategist predecessor, Supreme Allied Commander Dwight D. Eisenhower of World War II.

General Schwarzkopf commanded, managed, directed, oversaw, supervised, ruled, governed, and guided every phase of the war with Iraq. Of course he had much help, but even that is another example of the Strategist's natural leadership ability. He pulled together not only the right people and equipment but also other countries, giving them authority to handle their areas of responsibility.

This visionary leader could see in his mind's eye the outcome of the war from the very first day of battle, and he effectively set up an hour-by-hour, day-by-day, week-by-week strategy to reach the desired goal of victory for the allied forces, which he ultimately achieved.

In response to the general's positive reports of the war being "on schedule" to the desired victory, other Strategists went into action in the United States. Merchandisers produced and sold millions of every conceivable kind of imprinted item that bore Desert Storm slogans. "I Support Desert Storm," "These Colors Don't Run," "Norm for President," and other slogans flashed at us from badges, T-shirts, caps, bumper stickers, and cups. These calculators planned and executed highly profitable marketing strategies to capitalize on America's passionate emotional involvement in the war.

Although we have not actually tested the language communication style of General Schwarzkopf, as you study the traits of the Strategist in this chapter, we believe you will agree that there is little doubt his profile is clearly written here.

Vision of a Wall

Nehemiah was a beautiful example of a Strategist. He had a vision for rebuilding the broken-down walls of his hometown of Jerusalem. He began by asking the king's permission to do the project. He put himself under the proper authority. Then he organized the people, the plans, the supplies, the guards, and everything needed to rebuild the walls of the Holy City. Nothing could distract Nehemiah from his goal. He carried out his plan methodically, step-by-step, and soon accomplished his mission.

Although Nehemiah was born in exile, he grew up in the faith of Israel's God. He was the king's cupbearer and held a high place of honor in the palace in Shushan, having confidential access to the king.

For his patriotic task (Neh. 1:1–4) Nehemiah was well qualified. As a true Israelite, he labored for the purity of public worship, the integrity of family life, and the sanctity of the Sabbath. He was a soldier and statesman. He was courageous and God-fearing.

Alexander Whyte, in his essay on Nehemiah, admires him as a self-contained man, a man of his own counsel, a man with the counsel of God in his mind and in his heart. He was a resolute man, a man to take command of other men, a man in no haste or hurry. He did not begin until he counted the cost, and he did not stop until he finished the work. Tough conditions, adversity, character attacks, nonacceptance and other such circumstances will not control or cause a true Strategist who has a mission and a plan to give up. What an excellent description of a Strategist!

Open opposition and underhanded tactics were used to try to stop the work Nehemiah was doing for the Lord:

- Ridicule (Neh. 2:19; 4:2). But Nehemiah prayed that such a reproach might return to the reproachers, which it did (Neh. 4:4–6).
- Fear (Neh. 4:7–23). Enemies delivered an ultimatum, but Nehemiah set a watch so that swords and tools were united (Neh. 4:18).
- Guile (Neh. 6:2–4). Nehemiah knew that continuous conferences and discussions were useless and a waste of time; he refused to be distracted.
- False accusations (Neh. 6:5–9). He faced his accusors courageously because he had no selfish motives behind his endeavors, no hidden agendas; the accusations were unfounded. Truth gives one courage and confidence.
- Temptation to tempt God (Neh. 6:10–13). Nehemiah refused to hide himself in the temple as if he were doing wrong. His humbleness depended on God, who gave him strength.

Single-minded and single-hearted in his devotion to God and his work, Nehemiah was wise in his planning and in taking precautions against surprise attacks. He encouraged people who worked with him, and he was confident that God would fight for them.

Nehemiah organized and mobilized all the people around him; even the Jewish daughters were willing to take their places working along the damaged walls. As a result of his strategic leadership, he became governor of Jerusalem (Neh. 10:1). His greatest life accomplishment was the rebuilding of the walls, which remain as a monument to his great organizational abilities as a Strategist within the principles of God.

Strategists' Response to Life

Strategists think about what is happening. Then they cognitively examine their feelings. They generally do not feel their feelings in decision making as much as they do a mental checkup on their feelings. Finally, they act. After the action is complete, they may then allow themselves to feel their emotions, or they may not. They reason, plan, research, examine, and check feelings, then act, then feel.

Positive Characteristics of Strategists

Most Strategists probably automatically practice the habits discussed in Stephen Covey's book, *The Seven Habits of Highly Effective People.*

ORGANIZED AND EFFICIENT PLANNERS

Female Strategists plan their menus weeks in advance, plan dinner parties perfectly, are on time for everything, and expect others to be on time, also. Their houses, children, and families are organized and in perfect order. They organize PTA functions, church banquets, office parties, and charity balls. They seem to be able to keep a home and children running smoothly, *and* handle many activities or a full-time, probably high-pressure job outside the home.

Male Strategists' lives are planned with season tickets five years in advance. They plan vacations for the next several years. Their specific life goals and budgets are expressed in charts and spreadsheets. Like their female counterparts, they have many activities at home and at work, and they are capable of juggling them because of their ability to carefully organize and plan.

LONG-RANGE GOAL SETTERS

Strategists plan for today, next week, and next year. They have five-year, ten-year, and twenty-year goals. They even have a goal for how they want to be remembered after they are gone. Many of them have specific wills drawn that plan for every possible contingency.

VISIONARIES

Strategists have the ability to see, dream, and aspire. They can see the necessary steps, plans, resources, time, and people required to make the dream become a reality. They visualize the desired end result and all the details that must be put into place to achieve that result.

LEADERS OF PEOPLE

Strategists seem to instinctively know which person is best suited for which position. Whether it is at home, church, school, or work or in the community, they seem to be able to get the right people to do the needed jobs and activities. In situations where clearly no one is in charge, Strategists will size up the situation, gather facts, analyze the pros and cons, and then, if appropriate, assume responsibility and start planning and delegating. Unlike speakers of some languages, though, Strategists typically do not assume command out of selfish or egotistical power reasons. Rather, they want the entire group or program to succeed, and they can visualize what needs to be done to achieve success for everyone. For the most part, healthy Strategists gladly give credit for the success to the group and take little or none for themselves.

DELEGATORS

Delegating responsibilities to others is no problem for Strategists. They also have the patience and wisdom to follow through, check up, make sure others do their jobs, and see that others are qualified and trained. They enjoy delegating tasks and supervising people because they love to see others succeed. Not only do they see the jobs that need to be done, but they also seem to be able to discern who will be best suited for the task. Strategists understand and practice the leadership principle that "people defend what they work on." So, for a more dynamic administration, they give lots of individual members responsibilities to carry out so they have a sense of ownership.

GOOD AT DEVELOPING OTHERS

Strategists can place capable people in key positions, and they are good at teaching leadership principles. Whether in business or in child rearing, they train the older ones to care for the younger ones. Like polishing a piece of coal into a diamond, they can take people with undeveloped potential and turn them into crown jewels. In business, a true Strategist will usually move someone around from one position to another, trying to find where he is best suited rather than dismissing him for not performing well. When the person finally finds her niche, the Strategist is rewarded with outstanding service and loyalty.

ARTICULATE VERBAL COMMUNICATORS

Strategists are people people; yet they may at times seem aloof as they withdraw to think, plan, and schedule. They can express ideas clearly, and they easily talk about ideas, issues, concepts, and plans. However, they may not be especially good listeners as you share your ideas and plans. They also may have difficulty accessing and verbally expressing their feelings because they are more logically than emotionally tuned. The difference between these verbal communication skills and those of Influencers is that Influencers' overall style is enthusiasm out of a desire to relate and connect with others. Strategists seem to subconsciously desire to study human nature in order to learn how to work with and utilize people better. They enjoy the intellectual stimulation, but they do not necessarily require the emotional contact.

ACTION ORIENTED

Although this is primarily a cognitive language, Strategists are action oriented. They think about it, gather information, plan it, then do it. In contrast, speakers of the kinetic languages generally *do* before they plan.

ZEALOUS, SINGLE-MINDED, AND ENTHUSIASTIC

While Influencers are enthusiastic about almost everything, Strategists are enthusiastic about their project or projects and may have difficulty showing enthusiasm for your project if it is different from theirs.

UNCONCERNED ABOUT WHO GETS THE CREDIT

As long as the project or goal gets accomplished, Strategists typically do not crave the credit. They constantly keep their eye on the end result. As a matter of fact, they are prone to share the credit or give it to family, friends, the whole staff, or the entire team because they love to see people feeling useful and valuable. Since they usually have a lot of self-confidence, they do not need to be applauded to feel good about themselves. Their personal reward is the success of the project or program.

TALENT-AND-SKILL USERS

Strategists are able to use a person's talents and skills, even though that person's ethics and morals may contradict their own or the purpose of the project. Movers would have a more difficult time doing this. Strategists know the person's involvement often positively affects that person. In this way, Strategists often influence and attract people to God.

FUNCTIONAL UNDER AUTHORITY

As a natural flow of life, Strategists do not rebel at authority; they willingly submit. They expect persons under their authority to be cooperative, submissive, and not rebellious. As excellent leaders themselves, they realize that for any group or program to succeed, someone must be in charge, and others must be willing assistants and participants. When Strategists are in charge, they take charge, but when someone else is in charge, they gladly assist and participate, once again out of their desire to see things work smoothly and succeed.

EAGERNESS TO MOVE ON TO NEW CHALLENGES

Once something is completed, Strategists prefer to delegate the ongoing maintenance to others. Then they move on to new leadership goals and challenges that demand their planning and strategy abilities.

CONCERNED ABOUT APPEARANCES

Strategists seem to have it all together—not from an ego position but from their desire for excellence in all they do. They want to look their best. Both men and women do everything well. They want their children, homes, and businesses to reflect care and attention. As Christians, they desire to represent God through excellence in how they live, what they say, and how they act. They believe that things must *be* right and they must also *look* right to properly influence others.

Desires of Strategists

STRATEGISTS DESIRE TO REMOVE CHAOS AND CONFUSION FROM THE LIVES OF OTHERS BY MAKING THE WORLD A MORE ORDERLY PLACE THROUGH EFFICIENT, ORGANIZED LEADERSHIP AND PLANNING.

They want to look ahead down the road of life to see and avoid any potholes that would delay them or others on their way to the envisioned destination.

Possible Negative Characteristics of Strategists

DISLIKE OF TEAM LEADERSHIP

Born leaders, Strategists do not work well with team leadership or where they are allowed to move only with the consensus of a board of directors. They do not like to be involved in slow-moving committees. They can handle committed involvement if they are in charge, or if another person is in charge, but where no designated leader exists, the unproductive experience is very frustrating to them. They work better in solo leadership positions.

TENDENCY TO BECOME CALLOUSED AND SARCASTIC

Because leaders are the target of much criticism, Strategists can become somewhat calloused to protect themselves. That is why acceptance by their mates is so essential to the ongoing balance of Strategists. Continued criticism without offsetting affirmation may cause them to become critical and/or sarcastic in response and in self-defense.

WALLS OF SILENCE

Again to protect themselves, especially if the atmosphere is one of criticism, competition, or defensiveness, whether at home or in their businesses or social lives, Strategists may withdraw into their own private worlds.

PEOPLE USERS

To Strategists, the end result is sometimes worth the means, and they try to do whatever it takes to accomplish their goal, including using people inappropriately. They may act as though people are expendable or the feelings of others do not matter. Because they overlook their personal priorities to keep the overall project progressing, they expect others to do the same.

DRIVEN

To accomplish their goals, Strategists sometimes neglect their families and their own health. They can easily become workaholics to accomplish their all-important dreams and visions.

DIFFICULTY WITH ROUTINE JOBS

Strategists find routine jobs boring and without mental challenge. They tend to dislike dishwashing, dusting, yardwork, and housework, but they may feel guilty about it at the same time. However, they are good at delegating these uninteresting jobs to others. They do not mind projects, especially large-scale projects, but the daily routine of multiple small tasks drives them crazy. Strategists, therefore, often hire housekeepers, lawn care people, and other helpers to keep things looking good. Perhaps if you cannot afford to delegate it, and it still has to be done, you need to look at it as a big project rather than a routine job.

DEMANDING

Strategists tend to be perfectionists and demand perfection of others, with little or no regard to the fact that it is not the other person's God-given ability. They also tend to tell others what to do. They ask a lot of "Did you do this?" or "Did you remember to do that?" questions, which may feel like a put-down to the other person.

SEEMINGLY COLD OR INDIFFERENT

It is not that they *are* cold, indifferent, or uncaring, but because of their intense interest in goals, plans, details, and logical matters, Strategists may be perceived that way. Actually, their all-consuming interest in goals and plans helps others succeed and be happy.

UNWILLING TO ADMIT TO WRONG DECISIONS

The truth is, because of their great ability to gather facts and plan effectively, Strategists rarely are wrong. They do not get much practice admitting it. When they are really wrong, they first cannot believe it, then it is hard to admit it unless presented with irrefutable facts.

IMPATIENT

Strategists want things done as quickly as possible. They become impatient with delays and systems that do not operate on their time schedules. Strategists become impatient easily with people who are not logical, who do not share their goals, who get bogged down with indecision or lack of direction, or who have different priorities.

PERCEPTION OF THOSE CONTROLLED BY FEELINGS AS WEAK

Since this is a cognitive language, Strategists have difficulty understanding people who are controlled more by their emotions than by their logic.

EMOTIONALLY DISTRUSTFUL

Strategists get criticism from many sources since they are usually in the potshot position of leadership. They are often unwilling to trust others with their true feelings because they have probably been burned by doing so in the past.

> **DO NOT INTERPRET THEIR LACK OF EMOTIONAL EXPRESSION AS AN ACTUAL LACK OF EMOTION. STRATEGISTS ARE OFTEN AS EMOTIONALLY VULNERABLE AS PEOPLE OF OTHER LANGUAGES, BUT DUE TO THEIR EXPERIENCES AS LEADERS, THEY MAY BE GUN-SHY.**

Their mates can help them be more expressive by listening, encouraging them to express their feelings, and not criticizing them for how they feel.

RELUCTANT TO GO TO OTHERS FOR ADVICE OR COUNSEL

When Strategists need advice or counsel, they are reluctant to ask for it. If they do seek counsel, they then have a difficult time taking it unless it lines up with what they already know, want, or think. They also tend to think no one else could really understand because their situations are so different, so big, or so complicated. They feel that only God can help them.

Progressive Warning Signals of Distress

This predictive model indicates or predicts the sequence Strategists go through in times of normal to severe stress.

These are the Strategists' signals that show up in their lives when they are under stress and have not gotten their batteries charged in positive ways. This happens when unresolved issues emerge and reemerge from past hurts, toxic experiences, immaturity, stress, and lack of reliance on the Holy Spirit. The length and depth of the problems, and their failure to deal with them, determine the degree of negative distress signals. When these distress signals appear, Strategists dysfunction and sabotage their personal or professional lives in predictable ways:

- First-level distress warning signals. Strategists overdelegate or do it all themselves. They become demanding and drive self and others harder. They likely seem cold and indifferent.
- Second-level distress warning signals. They begin to use people; they are sarcastic, critical, and calloused.
- Third-level distress warning signals. They become suspicious, do not trust anyone, withdraw, become silent, and isolate themselves. They cut everyone else off, run away, and start over. They become addicted to amphetamines or exercise.

How Do I Love Thee?

AGREEMENT

Strategists experience love when their mates agree with the plans, purposes, visions, and goals of their lives. Their long-range and short-range goals need to correspond. Probably of the speakers of all the languages, Strategists look for agreement more than any of the others. They do not want unthinking agreement from a yes-person who does not have an opinion of his or her own, but they want agreement in shared values and vision.

> **THE STYLE OF STRATEGISTS IS A HIGHLY COMPETENT, USUALLY WELL-BALANCED LANGUAGE, AND IT IS EASY FOR OTHERS TO FEEL THREATENED BY THEM BECAUSE THEY ARE SO CAPABLE OF DOING SO MANY THINGS WELL.**

Being married to a Strategist can be especially difficult if you are somewhat insecure or tend to be competitive. Your spouse's many strengths might cause you to compare yourself to him or her and feel that you come up short. Keep in mind, though, that a Strategist would never want you to feel that way or to make such comparisons. Your spouse does not consider himself or herself better than you.

If you are married to a Strategist and you are healthy and mature enough to appreciate and encourage your mate to be all that God created him or her to be, and you allow your mate to express the natural leadership language, you will have a loyal, loving, and fantastic mate. Life will never be boring or mundane with a Strategist.

Strategists feel loved when you allow them to organize their lives, your life, the children, the home, the business, and "tomorrow the world." Maybe they would not go quite to that extent, but do not try to stop them at every turn or hold them back. God created them to be this way. Enjoy it!

These dynamic people feel loved when you give them your acceptance, making them feel included, worthy, and validated. Your acceptance validates their right to be here, to be who they are. By giving them acceptance, you are saying, "I recognize your significance in this world and in my life."

Because Strategists are born leaders, they are criticized a great deal, as all leaders are, from CEOs to teachers to football coaches to presidents of the PTA. At home a Strategist needs to feel accepted and nurtured by you to put balance back into life.

SPIRITUAL MOTIVATION

Each of the seven behavioral languages correlates to one of the motivational gifts listed in Romans 12:5–8. The Strategist's behavioral style generally correlates to the spiritual gift of leadership or administration. Each gift of grace is vital to the health and growth of the church, the body of Christ. Strategists organize and lead us dynamically in our quest for this life and the life to come.

FINANCIAL STYLE

When making investments, Strategists do not get emotionally involved or committed. We knew a Strategist who made investments for a group of Christian doctors. His investments were wise and profitable, and when we asked him how he did it, he explained that he did not allow himself to become emotionally involved with the investment. He said, for example, when a couple see a house that meets all the requirements that they want in a home, the preferred style, location, and the like, many will instantly get so emotionally attached to the house that they want it just because they love it. Maybe it is not the best deal in the world, but they rationalize that it is exactly what they want. Despite the need to fix the roof or foundation, they take it. Strategists will purchase the house only if it is a wise move, and they will not allow their emotions to control their financial decisions.

They spend or purchase wisely, work on a budget, and plan ahead ("in five years we will buy a boat"). They look for quality and the best price. They do not buy something just because it is a bargain if that compromises quality. If they have to sacrifice either quality or cost, they will pay more to buy the quality product, even though that means a delay in getting it so they can really afford it.

As in all areas of life, Strategists think, then act. When it comes to financial matters, they likely do not make the investment if it is not logical.

ENTERTAINMENT STYLE

Whether for large or small groups, Strategists entertain with grand perfection. Everything will be organized and ready. Nothing will be left to chance. For dinner parties there will be much food, choices of desserts, creative themes, and strategically arranged seating. Though they are comfortable with both large and small groups, these gatherings will not usually be spontaneous occasions. Their guest lists will be carefully planned. They have many friends, but they usually have only a few close friends that they feel they can trust, be themselves with, and feel accepted by. Strategists most enjoy having these people in their homes.

THE HOME

Strategists want things organized and efficient, but since they do not like routine jobs, these busy leaders need homes that work without a lot of upkeep on their part. They want their homes to be aesthetically pleasing, emotionally nurturing havens from the outside world. Whether a stately, ivy-covered home or one that is a more contemporary design, awards, certificates, and plaques are likely to be displayed because Strategists are so talented and have accomplished so much. Books and magazines will also reveal their interest in efficiency, organization, and management of time and people. Their homes tend to reflect the latest in energy-efficient appliances and equipment.

STRATEGISTS AND SEX

Strategists are not prone to have affairs. They control their expressions of emotions, and having sex outside marriage would not fit into their long-range spiritual goals. Strategists can get so organized and focused on other goals that they forget to stop and enjoy life, including having sex with their mates. They may need sexual reminders from their mates. However, once they are given an obvious reminder, they will emotionally and sexually respond and pursue excellence in all they do.

Because of their need for approval, Strategists need nurturing and reassurance. They need reminders that spouses are *for* them and that they can trust spouses. And because they can be verbal and action oriented, they need to be both told and shown that spouses love them dearly. Words and actions are vital to their living and understanding love.

Can This Marriage Be Saved?

Several years ago a couple came into our counseling office with a problem. The husband, Gary, could not understand why his wife, Janice, was so angry. He did all he could to make her life easier.

Every month he sat down at his computer and updated their nutritional needs as a family—what food each member needed the most, what vitamin supplements each was to take, menu plans, and grocery lists. Then he outlined their exercise schedule, and to further help his wife with her responsibilities, he outlined a schedule of her daily, weekly, and monthly duties for the next twelve months! Not only were those things outlined and scheduled, but she also had checks and measurements, such as time lines, reviews, and personal evaluations. All the things that worked in running his large electronics company, he instituted into his home life.

Each month Janice's personal confidence went down another notch, her anger grew, her resentment deepened, her hostility intensified, and finally, she realized that she was developing serious bitterness toward Gary. She felt inadequate, incompetent, and guilty. He was at a loss as to why she felt that way. All he was trying to do was make her life easier and do things to help her. She just would not get with the program. It was logical, it worked, it took away the unknown, and it was easy to follow. Just check things off as you go, and you always know where you stand in the big picture. "Plan your work and work your plan"—that was Gary's war cry.

Of course, Gary was speaking his language as a Strategist with no regard to her language as a Responder. Janice was not logical, organized, cognitive, or accomplishment oriented. She was gentle, sensitive, giving, and spontaneous, and she was perfectly capable of doing all that he wanted done. She just needed the freedom and support to do it her way.

A great deal of healing was needed for her to rebuild her self-esteem and confidence. It was hard for Gary to give up control and allow her to be who God created her to be, not who he was trying to re-create her to be. As we worked with them to see how their differences complemented each other and how God had obviously given them to each other to bring balance to their languages and lives, they began to see how much they needed each other. At last both stopped resisting and purposed to learn to accept, receive, and compliment each other. We are not saying it was easy for either of them, but with God's help, they are growing closer all the time. They are learning to appreciate each other's language differences, and each is accepting the other's weaknesses and strengths. They are bringing balance to each other.

A Strategic Close

The language of Strategists is a behavioral style that the rest of us should truly celebrate and thank God for. Without these visionary, organized leaders, our world would be in a chaotic mess going nowhere. These wonderful people envision and carry out worldwide programs of peace, progress, and relief. They are the unselfish planners and leaders who help us accomplish great goals, pursue magnificent dreams, and keep our eyes focused on our ultimate destination. These are God's people to lead us to the Promised Land.

> **HALF OF OUR MISTAKES IN LIFE ARISE FROM FEELING WHEN WE OUGHT TO THINK AND THINKING WHEN WE OUGHT TO FEEL.**
> **—JOHN CHURTON COLLINS**

Contemplator

Studious

Reflective

Peaceful

*As he thinks in his
heart, so is he.*
Proverbs 23:7

CHAPTER 7

Marching to a Different Drummer

LANGUAGE 4: CONTEMPLATORS

■

Fred and I (Anna) were sitting in our den relaxing as we always do after work. Fred was reading the paper, returning telephone calls, and talking to me. I was working on a project and talking to Fred. We were both watching television.

Our son, Michael, came into the den and sat down. "Hi, Son," we said and went right back to our routine, thinking he was now included in our conversation. Michael sat quietly for about ten minutes listening to us talk, watching us work, and ignoring the television. Finally, he got up and slowly walked out of the den and back to his room.

"What's the matter with him?" asked Fred.

"I don't know; maybe he's just tired," I said as we both went back to our talking, telephoning, reading, and watching.

Michael is a Contemplator. Unfortunately, we did not understand his language until he was about twenty years old, and he went through the first twenty years of his life competing with the television, the newspaper, the telephone, other people, and every project imaginable for our personal attention.

Contemplators need quality time and undivided attention to feel loved and important. Finally, once we began to understand Michael's style of communication, when he came into the den to spend time with us, we responded differently from the way we had before. We put down our newspapers, turned off the television, laid our projects aside, and postponed telephone calls until later. Sometimes, when we created the quiet atmosphere Michael needed, he opened up and shared his thoughts and activities with us. Sometimes we all sat quietly, not talking much but just being together. Quality just-for-me time with Michael showed our love for him.

Michael then began to understand and appreciate our more verbal and active languages. When he wants our attention, and we are both too busy talking and moving to notice, he has learned to say, "Time out. I need some quality time with you now," instead of walking away. All in all, our family has grown much closer from our working to pull down the behavioral language barriers between us. Each of us has a much deeper admiration and appreciation for the individual languages and communication styles of the others, and we are grateful to God for allowing us to learn this important aspect of our family relationship.

Before he and Anita got married, Michael contemplated thoughtfully where they would go on their honeymoon. Mexico? Hawaii? Orlando? No, too noisy and busy. He finally decided they would go somewhere by car so they could have quality time together, closing out all distractions, and be close together, just the two of them. No planes and no airports. No tourist attractions, amusement parks, or Broadway plays. No other people. Just them, close and romantic until they reached their destination.

Now, being a flamboyant Influencer type, I personally did not think that Amarillo, Texas, would have been my first choice for a great honeymoon. Fred (a Mover) and I would have chosen a place full of fun and adventure. Truthfully, though, Amarillo was the perfect choice for our Contemplator son and his new bride. It was seven peaceful, uninterrupted hours away from Dallas, providing an intimate atmosphere for two in which they could talk quietly and enjoy each other as they began their life together. They ultimately ended up in Santa Fe, New Mexico, where they hiked in the mountains, celebrated the sunsets, and had quiet, romantic dinners by candlelight.

A Converted Contemplator

Paul, the apostle, may very well have had the language of Contemplators as one of his primary languages. You may recall that immediately after his encounter with Jesus on the road to Damascus and his conversion to the Way, Paul left the country and spent three years in Arabia (Gal. 1:15–18) studying and learning about his newly chosen path. He was secluded where he could have quiet time to think through all the aspects of what had happened and the direction he wanted or needed to go in the future. When he returned from Arabia, he spent fifteen days of quality time with Peter, probably to further define his own role in the kingdom.

The letters of Paul also demonstrate his thinking nature. They are well planned, logical, and convincing. It is obvious that Paul spent much contemplative time preparing his arguments and statements to exactly fit his chosen audience.

Many authors, like Paul, are Contemplators. They require quiet time alone to think, plan, and then write. And what a dramatic impact some authors have had on our lives!

Contemplator types range from the college professors who quietly puff on their pipes before answering . . . to the strong, cowboy characters of our western movie heroes like Henry Fonda or Jimmy Stewart. Contemplators are found as great researchers, scientists, writers, inventors, high school teachers, or ministers.

Contemplators' Response to Life

Contemplators handle life and life's decisions by first thinking (reasoning, pondering, considering, analyzing, and observing). Then their feelings kick in. Next they pause, then they finally act.

Space and Contemplators

Each person occupies and uses a personal space or zone as if it were words. Contemplators usually require more space or privacy than speakers of other languages. They need time to be alone and to be alone with the Lord. Their spatial zones are clearly defined. They are selective about who they allow into their space. We all have spatial zones and use them, but how we communicate in and through them is not as important to others as to Contemplators. Therefore, it is a part of their behavioral language.

Each of us has personal territory, which is defined air space around the body. These air spaces are like portable bubbles, which are carried around with us, and their sizes usually depend on two factors. First, we are influenced by the density of the population in the place where we grew up. This personal zone is somewhat culturally determined. A person raised in a large family sharing a bedroom with a couple of brothers or sisters will typically have a much smaller spatial need than a person raised as an only child with his or her own room.

Second, people have definite spatial needs if their behavioral language is that of Contemplator. If you have a strong need for personal space, look and see if it is cultural or part of your natural God-given language as a Contemplator.

Positive Characteristics of Contemplators

PRIVATE

> **CONTEMPLATORS TEND TO PREFER A PRIVATE, RATHER THAN A PUBLIC, LIFESTYLE. THEY PREFER PEACE AND QUIET RATHER THAN NOISE, CONFUSION, AND HORDES OF PEOPLE. THEY LIKE TO AVOID LARGE CROWDS AND PREFER ONE-TO-ONE RELATIONSHIPS WHERE THEY CAN EXPRESS THEIR DEEP THOUGHTS AND BE HEARD ABOVE THE ROAR OF HUMANITY.**

PEACE LOVING

These quiet people are peaceful to be around, and they prefer peaceful, low-conflict situations. They do not like to confront others and will usually try to avoid confrontations. They will almost run from conflict, thinking this response preserves the peace.

THINKING BEFORE SPEAKING

Contemplators usually will not compete for attention or for the floor. They weigh their words, ponder their thoughts, and edit their speech in their minds before and while it comes out their mouths. This process reduces verbal blunders, but it also produces slower responses. They do not feel compelled to speak; they speak if and when they choose to do so. People who speak more quick-response languages sometimes interpret Contemplators' slower response time as also meaning they are slower mentally. Nothing could be more false. The truth is, before answering questions or expressing ideas, Contemplators analyze all the possibilities, check their facts, and organize their responses into usually logical, sequential answers. When they finally respond, the response will be worth hearing and will have been worth the wait.

MANY CONTEMPLATORS HAVE HIGHER-THAN-AVERAGE TO GENIUS IQS AND TEND TO HOLD JOBS THAT REQUIRE GREAT INTELLIGENCE. COLLEGE PROFESSORS AND PSYCHOLOGISTS OFTEN EXHIBIT THE CONTEMPLATOR BEHAVIORAL STYLE.

COMFORTABLE TEACHING OR PRESENTING

Like the apostle Paul, a Contemplator generally enjoys the spotlight of presenting to groups, regardless of size, so long as it is clear he or she is *the* presenter or lecturer. The presentation will obviously be well thought out and planned. You will always learn something valuable from a Contemplator.

WELL-DEFINED BOUNDARIES

All of us have invisible boundaries around us, which allow certain people and events in and out of our lives. These boundaries are usually weak, flexible, or rigid. Weak boundaries allow anyone and everything to absorb or control us (more of a problem for Influencers, Responders, and Doers). Flexible boundaries mean we can change, grow, and let people come and go in our lives as we choose, depending on our circumstances. Rigid boundaries mean we are usually closed, keep most people outside our lives, and do not seem to be able to change with situations, people, circumstances, or feelings. Flexible boundaries are the healthiest type, and Contemplators tend toward flexible to rigid ones. Strategists, Givers, Movers, and Contemplators have to be careful not to become too rigid.

STRUCTURED TIME

Like their Strategist cousins, Contemplators tend to structure their work, play, study, rest, free time, family time, and romantic time. Although they can choose to change their schedules and even choose to do something spontaneous, they prefer to schedule their activities and stick to their schedules. The schedules keep their lives orderly, quiet, and peaceful.

QUALITY TIME WITH FAMILY AND MATE

Special set-aside time together with family members is important to Contemplators. This is one of the ways they feel love and show love. These times do not need to be jammed with activities. Taking a quiet stroll in the park, reading a book together, or just sitting quietly next to another is all Contemplators need.

TIME ALONE

Contemplators *need* time and space alone. They have a strong need to withdraw from people and activities, and this time apart may or may not include mates. Mates must not take this need for aloneness personally.

> TOO MANY PEOPLE AND ACTIVITIES FOR TOO LONG AT A TIME DRAIN CONTEMPLATORS OF ENERGY AND HEALTH. LIKE RUN-DOWN BATTERIES, THEY MUST THEN BE SET ASIDE AND LEFT ALONE TO RECHARGE.

FOCUSING ON ONE THING BEFORE STARTING ANOTHER

Contemplators do not like to juggle multiple projects or relationships. People who speak the kinetic languages can get frustrated with Contemplators because they seem too slow. The truth is, Movers, Doers, and Influencers who are juggling four or five projects at once probably get them accomplished no faster than Contemplators who focus on one project, complete it, then go to another and complete it. Just as Contemplators do not want a life cluttered with activities and groups of people, neither do they want their minds cluttered with multiple projects. Such mental cluttering takes away their peace of mind and their ability to focus and give proper attention to each project in turn.

DEEP-THINKING, LOGICAL REASONERS

The observations and statements of Contemplators are often profound because they observe and think things through. They are intellectual and have great reasoning ability but not necessarily common sense. They naturally collect knowledge and information, not just surface facts. They want to know things in depth. When a friend of ours who is in graduate school gets her textbooks, she sits down and reads them through, wanting to know all that is within the covers not just to make good grades but to acquire knowledge. Contemplators love research and word studies.

VALIDATORS OF FACTS AND TRUTH

This trait especially shows up regarding spirituality. Contemplators desire to validate or authenticate the truth of God. Because of this, they do not accept a teaching or sermon at face value; they will look up the Scriptures on their own, they will ask the minister to explain, or they may even challenge a teacher on a point if they cannot find the truth or validation of the teaching.

> **CONTEMPLATORS SEARCH OUT AND INVESTIGATE THE TRUTH AS IF THEY ARE SPIRITUAL DETECTIVES.**

They accept rather slowly viewpoints or opinions of others.

> **PERHAPS THEY ARE SPIRITUAL DESCENDANTS OF THE BEREANS WHO "SEARCHED THE SCRIPTURES DAILY TO FIND OUT WHETHER THESE THINGS WERE SO" (ACTS 17:11).**

MARCHING TO THEIR OWN DRUMBEAT

> **CONTEMPLATORS ARE NOT CONCERNED OR CONTROLLED BY WHAT EVERYONE ELSE IS DOING.**

They can usually resist negative peer pressure, and they do not get caught up in the games of keeping up with others.

> **THEY REALLY DO NOT CARE WHAT THE JONESES ARE DOING NEXT DOOR OR ABOUT SOCIETAL TRENDS. THEY HEAR THEIR OWN DRUMBEAT, AND THEY MARCH TO THIS RHYTHM VERY WELL, PERHAPS COMPLETELY OUT OF STEP WITH OTHERS.**

LOYAL

Because they tend to hold on to the past, Contemplators are loyal to old friends, family, mementos, souvenirs, pets, and the like. Our son has always been very loyal, and we even noticed it years ago with our dogs. When Michael was growing up, we always had shelties (miniature collies); usually, we had a mature dog and a younger dog. Most children would have been caught up with the newness of the puppy, but Michael always stayed loyal and affectionate to the older dog. The little puppy was cute, but Michael's love and loyalty were with the older dog as long as she lived.

TENDENCY TO BE GOOD LISTENERS

Contemplators listen attentively; they do not interrupt, contradict, or confront. If they learn to give audible or visible responses to the speaker, they can be especially affirming to the person speaking.

ABILITY TO SEE THINGS FROM GOD'S PERSPECTIVE

These thinkers seem to be able to cut through the unimportant fluff of life, personal desires, and ambitions to see things as they really are, uncompromised in the value of biblical truth and godly principles. This ability gives them great spiritual insight for themselves and others, making them good counselors, ministers, educators, or businesspeople.

Desires of Contemplators

Contemplators desire to meet the intellectual needs of others. They are concerned about presenting all truth, especially biblical truth, in a logical, reasonable, rational, understandable way. They desire to overcome confusion and meet the needs of others through intellectual understanding.

Possible Negative Characteristics of Contemplators

TOO MANY INTERESTS

Contemplators may have trouble narrowing their wide range of intellectual and contemplative interests to a focused pursuit for a long enough period to be successful in a career. They may be job-hoppers or perpetual students. Mary, our coauthor, went to college with a man who had been a full-time student for nine years. He had changed his major many times just because he was so interested in so many different areas of study. Fortunately, his family was wealthy and could support his intellectual marathon journey. Unfortunately, he could never focus on an area long enough to become productive.

RELUCTANT TO SHOW OR SHARE FEELINGS

They tend to be the strong, silent type. Not only do Contemplators not *show* feelings, but they do not *share* them easily. As a matter of fact, they have a hard time accessing these feelings. This tendency can cause a bottling up of feelings, such as anger, depression, and fear. Emotional expression is difficult because Contemplators are more naturally adept at intellectual, logical reasoning.

Contemplators prefer to keep personal problems and feelings to themselves. Only those who have won their trust know them well. There are times when they do not easily share even with their mates, though, because Contemplators do not think about it and do not seem to realize that it is important. Once their mates get their attention, and they realize it is important, they will share, but they may have to be reminded again and again.

SENSITIVE

Although Contemplators can appear in control and somewhat stoic, they are usually quite sensitive and experience hurts and rejections easily. They just do not show it. Because of that, people may think that things do not bother Contemplators emotionally. They do.

LEGALISTIC

Contemplators can become legalistic and dogmatic in their interpretation of what is the pure truth, thinking that their viewpoints are correct because they have checked them out personally. They can also be dogmatic about their opinions or their memories of the past, believing that their recall is most accurate, which may or may not be true.

INFLEXIBLE

Contemplators are structured, especially in their thinking process, and it is difficult for them to be flexible, whether in accepting new ideas, new locations, new jobs, or new relationships. They like the security of consistency and sameness. Once they have put something into an appropriate mental cubbyhole, they want it to remain there undisturbed.

VISIBLY UNRESPONSIVE

Unless they have learned the importance of nodding to indicate understanding and listening or asking questions to keep conversations going, Contemplators will seem disinterested and uncaring.

FEELING OF REJECTION OR BEING SMOTHERED

Contemplators can be insecure in relationships, usually due to one or both of the following factors: the fear of rejection and/or the fear of being smothered. Although these may seem to be opposite concerns, both can be present within the same person, and both feelings can cause someone to avoid intimacy in order to avoid the rejection or smothering.

WITHDRAWAL OR ISOLATION/ABUSE

Contemplators need space, but if they are too demanding of space and act selfishly, they can cause mates and children to feel isolated, shut out, and unimportant.

One of our friends, Judith, was raised in a home where her father was a Contemplator. She grew up feeling alone, unimportant, emotionally isolated, and filled with shame. She did not understand that he was a Contemplator, and he did not realize the damage his withdrawal and thoughtless demands for space did to his daughter. By the time we met Judith, her father was quite old, but it was still not too late for them to find a new level of understanding. When she understood that he was a Contemplator and that his quiet need for space was not meant to make her feel isolated or unimportant, she wept. The more she studied about the personality of the Contemplator, the more she was overcome with deep love and compassion for her father. When they got together the next time, Judith and her father had a warm reunion and the beginning, at last, of a relationship of acceptance and caring.

EXCLUSIVE RATHER THAN INCLUSIVE

Contemplators' friends, families, and coworkers may feel left out of their lives, slighted, or neglected. They tend to segregate their relationships and not commingle them. Though this tendency is not all bad, others need to understand it so they will not take it personally. And Contemplators need to understand it so they can be sensitive to the feelings of others and not make them feel abandoned, neglected, or left out.

PRIDEFUL

Developing their intellectual abilities can cause Contemplators to be impatient or prideful or to look down on people who do not share their reasoning skills. It is important for them to remember that their contemplative natures and IQs are gifts from God, who would not have them feel superior to His other creations.

> **HUMILITY IS A HALLMARK OF CONTEMPLATORS' MATURITY.**

UNCOMFORTABLE OR BORED WITH CASUAL CONVERSATION

Contemplators do not usually participate very long in superficial talk. After a little while, they disengage themselves either physically or mentally. They enjoy quality conversation and are able to discuss many different subjects because they have accumulated many facts and much information. At social chitchat, though, they may seem awkward and tend to treat it as a waste of time, which can be confusing to others, even causing them to experience rejection.

TENDENCY TO FRUSTRATE OTHERS WITH FACTS

Excited about new facts and knowledge, these thinkers may go into great detail sharing information with others, overwhelm them, and go way beyond their point of interest. For instance, you may ask, "Can you use this program on the computer?" Contemplators will tell you about the computer's drive, its megabytes, RAM, speed, and other related features, when all you wanted was a simple yes or no.

SLOW TO SPEAK OR RESPOND

Because Contemplators think things through so thoroughly, they are slow to speak, act, or respond. This delay can be exasperating and frustrating to others, such as Movers, Doers, and Influencers, who want Contemplators to be on their timetables. On top of the delay, their response may not seem appropriate because it is a deeper and more complex answer than is expected. Doers, Movers, and Influencers will be saying to themselves, "Just get on with it!"

GOOD, BUT UNUSUAL SENSE OF HUMOR

Contemplators seem to have a somewhat unusual sense of humor that others may not fully understand. Their sense of humor may be considered dry, philosophical, and complex, but it may seem so off the wall, missing the point, or bizarre that you think they are simplistic or immature. Days later you may come to realize what they meant and be amazed and amused by it. Keep an open mind and listen carefully when Contemplators are talking or being funny—you will invariably learn something significant.

Progressive Warning Signals of Distress

This predictive model indicates or predicts the sequence Contemplators go through in times of normal to severe stress.

These signals show up in Contemplators' lives when they are under stress and have not gotten their batteries charged in positive ways. That is when unresolved issues emerge and reemerge from past hurts, toxic experiences, immaturity, stress, and lack of reliance on the Holy Spirit. The length and depth of the problems, and their failure to deal with them, determine the degree of negative distress signals. When these distress signals appear, Contemplators dysfunction and sabotage their personal or professional lives in predictable ways:

- First-level distress warning signals. Contemplators display low self-confidence, begin to withdraw, and become prideful, legalistic, and critical.
- Second-level distress warning signals. They remain critical, begin self-justification and denial, and become defensive and inflexible.
- Third-level distress warning signals. They begin feeling overwhelmed, invaded, controlled, smothered, rejected, and unloved. They then become more critical and judgmental, and they deny their responsibility. They push others away, withdraw, drop out, and inflict isolation abuse on others.

How Do I Love Thee?

ATTENTION

CONTEMPLATORS FEEL LOVED WHEN YOU GIVE THEM PERSONAL ATTENTION. THEY NEED BOTH QUALITY TIME AND UNDIVIDED ATTENTION.

Saying "I love you" as you run out the door while grabbing your briefcase, feeding the dog, looking for your keys, and pouring a cup of coffee does not make a Contemplator feel loved. Having a quiet, unhurried visit with a focused, sincere, allotted time to just say "I really love you" is needed. Focusing on them and them only is a key to loving and working with Contemplators because whatever they are involved in gets their undivided attention. They feel loved when you make plans for special moments or do extra work so you can spend quality time with them. They like taking long walks, holding hands, having quiet dinners, sharing projects, playing board games, and doing activities with their mates.

They also feel loved when mates allow them time they need alone or apart. Contemplators know that this is an unselfish act and really appreciate the allowance and the aloneness mates give them.

They need reassurance from their mates that their fears of rejection are unfounded. They also need reassurance that they will not be smothered or absorbed, especially if they are married to a mate like a Mover or Doer who speaks a more assertive language.

Contemplators are sensitive, although they have difficulty expressing many emotions, and for them to feel loved, this sensitivity must be acknowledged and handled gently.

SPIRITUAL MOTIVATION

Each of the seven behavioral languages correlates to one of the motivational gifts listed in Romans 12:5–8. The Contemplator's behavioral style generally correlates to the spiritual gift of teaching. Each gift of grace is vital to the health and growth of the church, the body of Christ. Contemplators study and teach us the Word of God to guide our lives and hearts.

FINANCIAL STYLE

Contemplators usually have a well-planned, well-thought-out system for handling their finances. However, because they think, then feel rather rapidly, their feelings may bump aside their logic in buying habits. They can purchase impulsively, sometimes foolishly, or even sometimes overspend. They usually have a budget, but because of their impulsive purchasing, they may ignore the budget. However, when they do overspend, they tend to get back on track and get back on the budget. They really desire and appreciate the best, highest quality name brands at good prices, and they are willing to shop and look until they find them.

ENTERTAINMENT STYLE

When it comes to entertainment, Contemplators' first preference is their mates, then their families, then small intimate groups with a few select friends. Naturally, their entertaining is centered on quality, set-aside time. Contemplators enjoy entertaining with their spouses and working together to bring it all about. They like playing card games and board games, participating in Bible studies and discussions, watching movies, reading, listening to music together, and sitting by fireplaces. They are often musically talented and are comfortable sharing and entertaining using their talent.

THE HOME

Contemplators' homes will be cozy and filled with special things. They tend to keep things from childhood, school years, and trips they have taken. They usually have many pictures of special times with others. Their homes will truly reflect their personal history and tastes rather than the latest look in decor. They like for their homes to be conducive to intellectual stimulation, with computers and lots of books and research material for studying, reading, and conversation.

CONTEMPLATORS AND SEX

Contemplators are sensitive and attentive lovers. They like the specialness of the moment, and they invest quality time, thought, and feelings in sexual experiences with their mates. Contemplators may be difficult to converse with at times, but they make up for it by being responsive and sensitive sexual communicators. The Contemplator husband tends to be patient and gentle with his wife to make her feel very special and loved. The Contemplator wife will be very attentive to her husband and will let him know that he is preferred and revered.

Are Contemplators susceptible to sexual temptation? When they are operating in their intellectual, logical, and analytical mode, no. It would not be a logical or practical thing to do. However, many times college professors, psychologists, counselors, or ministers who are Contemplators fall into this temptation trap if there is exposure to temptation along with the denial of their vulnerability and neediness (pride). They usually are safe from giving in to this temptation because of their love of biblical truths and principles. Also, close, harmonious, and covenant marriages with mates, who purpose to stay close and attentive to them, will keep Contemplators out of harm's way.

Married to a Contemplator

After we gave a seminar on the behavioral languages, a woman approached us in tears. We sat down to talk with her, and she shared this story.

Joanne was in her second marriage. She was married a number of years ago, was single a few years, and had been happily married to Charles for about five years. Her tears were from understanding and relief. She was still recovering from the insecurity and fear she had experienced from her first marriage and the divorce.

Joanne told us that was the first time she had ever understood what had happened in her relationship with her first husband, Robert. She now recognized he was a Contemplator. Had she understood his language, the marriage might still have ended, but she would not have had all those years of guilt, grief, rejection, resentment, and confusion.

From what Joanne shared, Robert had more of the negative qualities of Contemplators than the positive. Still, had she understood that, she would not have taken them so personally. He withdrew, isolated himself from her, would not communicate, was unresponsive and inflexible, and resisted change. He was very sensitive, yet he could not show his feelings to her. Robert was legalistic and thought *his* way was the *only* way. During their marriage he had been both a minister and a professor.

Joanne was a Responder, who thought all his problems were her fault. She assumed responsibility for his unhappiness and her unhappiness, and she kept trying harder and harder, which resulted in her feeling more and more guilty and depressed.

Joanne told us at the seminar, "Tonight, for the very first time, I feel fully released. I now understand that Robert's problems were not my fault. I have no reason to ever allow Satan to put that guilt trip back on me." We prayed with her that the Lord would complete her healing, to know that she was forgiven by God, and that she could now fully forgive herself. We then asked her present husband, Charles, to join us. He was thrilled with Joanne's understanding of the past and the release that she had received. As they sat with their arms around each other, tears rolling down their cheeks, we prayed for God to fully bond them to each other. We prayed that whatever had been given away in other relationships would be restored to them and that they would truly and completely be one flesh, sealed with a seal that could never be broken. They committed to be sensitive to one another and to become fluent in each other's language.

Thinking It Through

> **AS YOU LISTEN TO THE INTERTWINING RHYTHMS OF LIFE AROUND YOU, BE SURE TO KEEP A FINE-TUNED EAR FOR THE COUNTERBEAT THAT CONTEMPLATORS ADD TO THE SYMPHONY. THEY DO MARCH TO A DIFFERENT DRUMMER, BUT THAT BEAT IS THE STEADY, CALMING, CONSISTENT BEAT THAT ADDS PEACE AND CONTENTMENT TO LIFE.**

Celebrate God's Contemplators and their deep and gentle influence on our world.

> **A PERSON OF MEDITATION IS HAPPY, NOT FOR AN HOUR OR A DAY, BUT QUITE ROUND THE CIRCLE OF ALL HIS OR HER YEARS.**
> **—ISAAC TAYLOR**

Giver

Generous

Thoughtful

Responsible

God loves a cheerful giver.
2 Corinthians 9:7

CHAPTER 8

Thinking of You

LANGUAGE 5: GIVERS

■

Everyone agreed. The church needed a larger building. The members had been agreed for a long time, but every time they got together to discuss the project, all sorts of disagreements sprung up about how to build it and exactly what kind of building to construct. The minister was at his wit's end and appointed a day of prayer for the members to ask God's help in resolving the matter.

As the *Sunday School Times* went on to tell, very few of the church members attended the prayer service, but one devout woman went and took her five-year-old daughter. As they prayed, the little girl began to understand that it was about building a new church building. When they got home, she asked many questions about the new building, and then she became very quiet.

The next morning the mother could not find the little girl and, in a frenzy, went to look for her. It was not hard to follow her tiny footsteps through the snow to the minister's house. When the mother arrived, there in the front yard was little Mary with her toy wheelbarrow. In the wheelbarrow were two bricks. She was talking to the pastor, and tears were running down his cheeks. Mary had brought the two bricks as her gift to start the new church building.

On the following Sunday the minister told the story of Mary's very special gift. Her gentle generosity touched the hearts of the older members with repentance, and soon little Mary's two bricks multiplied into a beautiful new church building. Little Mary was a Giver, and "God loves a cheerful giver."

Keep On Giving Anyway

"The Lord told me to give this to you," whispered Francis as he handed me an envelope. Then he returned to his seat across the room next to his wife, Catherine.

Opening the envelope, we found a check made out to our counseling ministry in a substantial amount. And it was not the first time that Francis and Catherine had blessed our work with such gifts of love. They are both Givers, and giving is their primary means of communication with others. It is their language of love.

We call Francis and Catherine our spiritual parents because they prayed so earnestly for us during those early rocky years of our marriage when we were not living for the Lord. They barely knew us, but they had a real burden for us. After we committed our lives and marriage to the Lord, these special friends nurtured, spoon-fed, and loved us into the emotional healing that we needed in our family. They know about loving and giving; they have been married over fifty years.

Through those years, Francis and Catherine have served the Lord through their unselfish giving to others. They have paid scholarships for kids to go to Bible college, taken many people to the Holy Land, helped build church buildings and Bible schools, given numerous major pieces of equipment to ministries and churches, and so much more. The list of their gifts to others would fill this book.

Usually a successful businessman, Francis lost everything in the late 1960s. Still, he and Catherine kept on giving well above the biblical example of 10 percent. They would never think of giving less. As they remained faithful in their giving through troublesome times, God honored them by restoring more than they had lost. The time came when they were giving around 50 percent of their total income to the work of the Lord. Funny thing, the more they gave, the more they received. (Does this sound like Job of old?)

Great Givers, Francis and Catherine are also great receivers. No matter what we give them, whether great or not-so-great, to them it is always "just right" or "exactly what we wanted." Catherine almost dances across the room with excitement, even over mundane gifts. True Givers, you see, are also truly grateful and gracious receivers.

As some of our best friends, Francis and Catherine often share their home with us. In fact, they share their home with everybody who comes along! They love having guests in their home every weekend, and they have had many people stay in their home through the years. Each person is treated with the same hospitality, dignity, warmth, and joy.

Givers like Francis and Catherine are truly blessings from the Lord to the rest of us. We need more of them in this world, and this is a behavioral language that all of us should strive to become fluent in speaking.

Giving Your All

The most remarkable story of a Giver in the Bible is, ironically, about the smallest gift perhaps ever given. The gift amazed and astonished even Jesus Himself, who watched as a widow unselfishly gave her last two mites to God. A mite was a tiny copper coin worth less than a penny, and in our society today we might think, *That's no big deal.* Jesus thought otherwise.

Luke 21:1–4 reveals the incident and Jesus' reaction this way:

> And He looked up and saw the rich putting their gifts into the treasury, and He saw also a certain poor widow putting in two mites. So He said, "Truly I say to you that this poor widow has put in more than all; for all these out of their abundance have put in offerings for God, but she out of her poverty put in *all the livelihood that she had*" (emphasis ours).

The amazing part of this story is not the amount of the gift, as you can see. The truly amazing part is the widow's heart for giving—the only money she had left to live on. Jesus thought so, too. And what an incredible impact that selfless woman has had through the centuries! Hundreds of years later the story of her two-mite gift is still being told and retold to inspire us to be as giving in heart and attitude as she was.

Philanthropists

Givers are the generous philanthropists of our world. In their hearts is a sincere love for people. Their love is manifested in gifts, such as donations of money, property, jobs for jobless people, food to hungry people, clothes to needy people, and in so many other ways.

CHRISTIANS WITH THE GIFT OF GIVING TRULY
UNDERSTAND THAT EVERYTHING THEY HAVE IN
THEIR POSSESSION IS ONLY ON LOAN FROM GOD. HE
HAS ENTRUSTED CERTAIN OF HIS BELONGINGS TO US
IN THE HOPE THAT WE WILL HANDLE THEM AND
DISPENSE THEM IN THE SAME UNSELFISH WAY THAT
HE WOULD.

Because that concept is crystal clear to Givers, they are more than willing to share what they have with anyone who needs it. In fact, it makes them happy to do so.

Our friend Marte, a businesswoman, is another of God's gracious Givers. She exemplifies the openhearted giving characteristic of God: you cannot outgive God, and it is difficult to outgive Marte. She sends thank-you gifts, gifts for every special occasion, and gifts for no particular reason at all. Not only is she generous and thoughtful with the gifts she buys, but many times she will take something that is one of her favorite possessions and give it to someone else, regardless of its value.

Marte has, from time to time, given away most of the clothes in her closet to someone who wears her size because she felt that the Lord wanted her to meet the need. We have known her in times of plenty and in times of little, and her generosity always remains the same. One of the great principles we have learned from Marte is that

GOD DOES NOT CARE SO MUCH WHAT WE OWN, BUT
HE DOES CARE ABOUT WHAT OWNS US.

So, when things start to become too important to Marte, she believes it is time to release them, share them, and pass them on so that they can bless others and so that she will not be owned by or in bondage to them.

True to His nature, as Marte gives, God gives her even more so that she can give even more. She is a glorious example of God's promise: "Give, and it will be given to you: good measure, pressed down, shaken together, and running over will be put into your bosom. For with the same measure that you use, it will be measured back to you" (Luke 6:38).

Givers' Response to Life

Giving is a thinking language. When Givers respond to life events, they first access their cognitive, logical ability. After careful thought, Givers then use their feelings to evaluate their response. Finally, they move on to the appropriate action.

People often think that God's appointed Givers give through emotions, but this is first a cognitive language. Only after they think, consider, ponder and, of course, pray do they access their feelings, and then act.

Positive Characteristics of Givers

UNDERSTANDING THAT ALL COMES FROM GOD

Givers seem to understand that truly God gives us wisdom to get wealth, and it is not of ourselves. Whether they have money, possessions, or material things, and even if they worked hard for them, Givers understand that all these blessings are from the Lord.

THOUGHTFUL

Givers speak one of the most thoughtful languages. Givers consider others, like to find out their likes and dislikes, and remember little things about others. They learn the preferences of others, then remember to give gifts accordingly. Givers are wonderful to have as friends because you know that their gifts will be things you really like. Through the years, our friends Francis and Catherine have blessed us with everything from silk flowers that are the perfect color for a spot in the living room to books by our favorite authors to sweaters, pen and pencil sets, or music that reflects a great deal of thought and personal consideration. They do this for each of their friends. They choose gifts to meet each person's individual taste.

GENEROUS

Givers are generous with their time, talents, and material goods. They share their money, and they like to do things for others.

Givers like to give gifts to others. They buy gifts for all occasions and for no occasion. Their gift giving is their way of saying, "You're special, and I was thinking of you." They truly believe it is more blessed to give than to receive.

PLANNERS

Givers are almost never caught off guard. They always have items on hand to give for birthdays, showers, anniversaries, retirements, and other times. They also buy specific gifts ahead of time. Always prepared, not just with gifts but with most things, their freezers are almost always filled with food items ready for unexpected company.

GRATEFUL

True Givers are grateful for all they have. They seem to have grateful spirits, which generally give them joyful outlooks on life. Their grateful spirits help to keep them healthy, as Dr. Karl Menninger, founder of the Menninger Clinic in Kansas and author of *Whatever Became of Sin*, said,

> **"GIVING IS A GOOD CRITERION OF A PERSON'S MENTAL HEALTH. GENEROUS PEOPLE ARE RARELY MENTALLY ILL."**

GOOD STEWARDS OF POSSESSIONS

Givers prefer to buy quality merchandise, and they take good care of what they have. They are not careless, and they expect their things to last. Because they are grateful for what they have, they treat things with respect and care.

GIVERS OF THE BEST

Whether they are giving to God with their tithes and offerings, to people they love, or to people they have never met, Givers try to always give their best. They do not keep the best for themselves and give away what they do not like or need. They seem to understand that giving to others is a Christlike quality, and they want to give the best they have in honor of Him.

DELIGHT IN MEETING MATERIAL NEEDS

While speakers of other languages are more concerned about the emotional or intellectual needs of others, Givers like to make life easier or more pleasant and gracious for others by meeting material needs. They are especially blessed when they give to someone and later find out that it was a prompting of the Lord, and their generosity was an answer to that person's prayer.

GOOD-TO-EXCELLENT MONEY MANAGERS

We may think Strategists would naturally be the best handlers of finances or accounting items, but the best natural money managers are probably the Givers. They shop for best buys and invest wisely for the best return on their money. They are not foolishly extravagant or compelled to buy, invest, or give in response to an immediate emotional whim. As a matter of fact, they know there are always needs around them. They seem to give when God tells them, when it is appropriate, or when they know that their giving will be *the* answer to a problem or prayer. They do not give just because someone hurts.

RESPONSIBLE

Givers are very responsible, which is a necessary companion to their generous quality. Otherwise, they would be generously irresponsible. They give wisely and prayerfully. This responsibility also makes them excellent friends, employees, managers, and financial leaders.

GRACIOUS AND GIFTED AT ENTERTAINING AND HOSPITALITY

When they entertain, Givers make everyone feel at home and special. They pay attention to the least detail so their guests can tell that they have given much thought to the event. They are always well prepared. Even when they do something on the spur of the moment, it comes across so perfectly that guests feel that it was planned. Others feel special in their homes or offices.

Giving and hospitality go together, as Givers seem to quite naturally give through their hospitality. They are not the hosts and hostesses who are so formal everyone is uncomfortable. They are entirely gracious, and this graciousness extends to everyone—old friends to new acquaintances. All are treated with joy, respect, dignity, and love.

No Expectation of Personal Reward from Giving

The basic nature of Givers is to feel privileged to give to others, and they do not do so with a desire for personal reward. Emotionally healthy, mature Givers expect nothing in return.

Well-Rounded

> **SPEAKERS OF ALL THE LANGUAGES ARE SPECIAL AND UNIQUE, WITH MANY STRENGTHS AND WEAKNESSES, BUT OVERALL GIVERS SEEM AMONG THE MOST WELL-ROUNDED, WELL-BALANCED, AND MULTITALENTED OF THE BEHAVIORAL STYLES.**

Desires of Givers

Givers love to meet the material needs of others. Sensitive to the prompting of the Lord, they often respond to needs that have never been mentioned. It is not uncommon for Givers to walk up to someone they may not know, hand over a check, and find out later that it met a specific need the person had been praying about to God.

Possible Negative Characteristics of Givers

Strings Attached to Giving

If Givers are not emotionally mature, they might give with impure motives to control another or to get something in return. Sometimes this giving is seen with their children, family members, or friends.

Those who speak this language are encouraged to guard their hearts to make sure their motives are pure, so their giving will bring glory to the Lord.

Tendency to Bribe Others

Givers must be aware of the difference between the positive motivation of rewards and the negative motivation of bribery.

Rewards are given to someone in recognition of doing something worthwhile. The pure reward benefits the receiver and not the Giver. Bribery, on the other hand, is a control or manipulation factor and is used to get someone to do something to benefit the Giver.

MATERIALISTIC

Givers may become materialistic and use their abilities to gather materialistic goods and then keep them. These Givers will never find genuine happiness because they are polluting God's gift. They have been endowed with the gift of giving in order to serve and bless others. When they use it to heap things on themselves, they are not operating in the will of God.

TENDENCY TO CONTROL USE OF GIFTS

For example, if Givers give money to build a new wing on a church building, they want to tell you how to build it, what style, or what materials to use. They may give money to a friend who is having financial problems, then they want to tell him how and where to use the money. True, noncontrolling Givers give to the person or need and release it. No strings are attached.

OTHERS PRESSURED TO BE GIVERS

Most people want others to speak their languages, but this is especially true of Givers. They do not understand why others do not give the way they do. So, they apply pressure to force, enlighten, or inspire others to give. They say things like, "I would never go shopping and just buy things for myself. I always bring home something for my family or something for gifts." And generally they do, so they may say that with a little pride. Or it could be self-pity that says, "You left me out, and I always get something for you." They do not understand how others can be selfish and buy only for themselves.

CONSIDERED FOOLISH AND UNPREDICTABLE

Givers may be following the leading of the Lord and give abundantly to someone or to some cause. If others do not speak the giving language, especially Doers who speak a more practical language, they may see Givers as extravagant or unwise. However it may look, Givers have usually thought through the gifts, and they are confident that their giving is appropriate. Seldom do true Givers follow only their emotions. Theirs is a cognitive language, and they gather facts and weigh matters carefully before acting.

TENDENCY TO SPOIL CHILDREN OR OTHERS

Because Givers love to give, they may give so much that it spoils others. They have to learn to use restraint so that the giving does not lose its meaning or so that others do not begin to expect Givers to give to them.

BUYING WAY OUT OF RESPONSIBILITY

At times it is more appropriate to give self and personal efforts than money. Givers may be more comfortable giving money or gifts than personal effort, and they may use money as the easy way out. This giving is more impersonal and may not take as much time. Mature Givers seem to know when to give money, when to give time, and when to give personal involvement of self. They do not have just one method of giving.

PERFECTIONISTIC IN ENTERTAINING

Givers' need for perfection in entertaining can put demands both on Givers and on family members, causing stress and pressure in their homes. Mates and children may feel that they are less significant than the occasion or the guests, which lowers self-esteem in the family. This perfectionistic tendency can also cause others to feel that they never quite measure up to Givers' expectations.

FAMILY MEMBERS MINIMIZED

Because so much effort goes into making guests feel special, if Givers are not mature and careful, their children and spouses can feel that they are here just to serve the guests. Mature Givers make their families feel the most special of all.

USE OF GIFTS TO OBTAIN FAVOR, FRIENDSHIPS, OR INFLUENCE

All the languages have negative qualities, and no one is pure and perfect all the time. However, it seems that the negative qualities of Givers are some of the easiest to recognize. When Givers use their money or gifts to win favors, to procure friendships, or to win positions of influence, it may work for a season, but it does not give life to either Givers or their receivers. This ungodly pattern can lead to many problems.

Progressive Warning Signals of Distress

This predictive model indicates or predicts the sequence Givers go through in times of normal to severe stress.

Givers show certain signals in their lives when they are under stress and have not gotten their batteries charged in positive ways. That is when unresolved issues emerge and reemerge from past hurts, toxic experiences, immaturity, and lack of reliance on the Holy Spirit. The length and depth of the problems, and their failure to deal with them, determine the degree of negative distress signals. When these distress signals appear, Givers dysfunction and sabotage their personal or professional lives in predictable ways:

- First-level distress warning signals. Givers become critical and materialistic, and they use people inappropriately.
- Second-level distress warning signals. They become judgmental and control others through money, bribes, and strings attached to their gifts.
- Third-level distress warning signals. Givers finally become stingy, selfish, and even more controlling. They buy their way out of responsibility and tend to abandon people if they are not living or managing life according to the Givers' standards and opinions. They may also become emotionally abusive to those who are close to them. They will withdraw, isolate themselves, and hoard things of real value, potential value, or imagined value.

How Do I Love Thee?

APPRECIATION

Givers feel loved when their gifts of love are appreciated, which makes them feel appreciated, as they see their gifts as an extension of themselves.

When Givers receive gifts from their mates, they feel loved when the gifts reflect thought and attention. They do not respond to last-minute, grab-it-as-you-run gifts. The cost is not what makes them feel loved, although quality is important to them. It is the depth and sensitivity of thought that truly counts. They appreciate gifts for all occasions and for no occasion—gifts that just say, "While I was away from you, I was thinking of you, and this gift is an expression of my thoughts of love."

Givers also feel loved when their gifts are appreciated. As a matter of fact, they like for you to love their gifts and be excited about them. When you do not show excitement, they feel like failures, and their egos take a real blow.

Givers love for their homes to reflect hospitality, and you will make your Giver mate feel happy and loved when you participate in sharing the hospitality of your home with others.

SPIRITUAL MOTIVATION

Each of the seven behavioral languages correlates to one of the motivational gifts listed in Romans 12:5–8. The Giver's behavioral style obviously correlates to the spiritual gift of giving. Each gift of grace is vital to the health and growth of the church, the body of Christ. Givers bless our lives with examples of generosity and kindness.

FINANCIAL STYLE

> **PROBABLY OF THE SPEAKERS OF ALL THE LANGUAGES, GIVERS ARE THE VERY BEST AT HANDLING FINANCES.**

Even though Strategists use thought and wisdom in handling finances, Givers are usually more naturally gifted to deal with money, investments, or finances. Many seem to have a gift for making money, which goes with their ability to gather material goods. They usually have a strong and varied monetary portfolio, with amounts in savings, CDs, stocks, and real estate.

> **GIVERS KNOW THAT TO GIVE, THEY MUST MAKE AND HAVE, THEN THEY CAN SHARE.**

Although they typically buy ahead of time, not at the time of the need, they shop wisely, buy with thought and deliberation, seek out good buys or bargains, and are not extravagant. Yet, true Givers like to give the best, so they buy and give quality. Many times we find Givers as bookkeepers, accountants, financial planners, and financial officers.

ENTERTAINMENT STYLE

The Giver's home is usually one where everyone loves to go. Givers are always prepared for drop-in guests or emergencies. And they love to entertain either small or large groups. They usually have more than an abundance of food. Givers never seem to run out.

A great deal of thought and planning goes into the Giver's entertaining. Well-planned menus and guest lists, decorated table settings and centerpieces, and well-thought-out party themes are typical of Givers. Givers often give each guest a favor or a little wrapped gift.

When Givers have Bible studies or fellowship gatherings in their homes, they like to think the event through, have a plan, and give instructions even before it happens. We have some Giver friends who recently had their couples' prayer group in their home for New Year's Eve. The wife asked each person to bring the Bible verse that had been the most meaningful during the last year. Then they were to be in prayer throughout the evening as to who the Lord would have them give that verse to as a personal gift for the coming year. This gift giving was followed by delightful and delicious gourmet food, several coffees, teas, punch, and rich desserts in the comfort of a home that seemed to say, "Welcome! We're so glad you're here and would like for you to stay as long as you want."

It is a blessing to be invited into the home of a Giver.

THE HOME

Givers really want their homes to be places to share with others. They love to have fellowships, Bible studies, and surprise dinners so they can give of their hospitality. When a friend's mate is out of town, they will invite the family over for dinner. They have the boss, the minister, and the neighbors in and welcome them with warmth and love. Their homes are usually places of peace, orderly or well organized. Givers seem to have good taste in decorating and a flair for making homes inviting.

GIVERS AND SEX

Givers will see their marital relationships as opportunities to give, and this attitude will usually extend to their sexual relationships with their mates. This is first of all a cognitive language, but that is closely followed by their feelings, and they like to show love, care, and concern. They make their mates feel loved and cherished by being sensitive to the intimate needs of their mates. They desire to meet or respond to their mates' needs by giving whatever their mates require.

Givers can become overextended if they have not developed healthy boundaries. They generally think things through first, and keep their emotions in check so they resist temptation better than most types.

Giving Up?

One of the most interesting combinations in marriage is the joining of a Giver and a Doer, as exemplified in a couple we counseled named Dennis and Sheryl. Their marriage had deteriorated to the point that they shared only stress, tension, and anger. Neither understood his or her own behavioral language, much less the language of the other. Both of them were almost exclusively operating from their negative language characteristics rather than their positive ones.

Dennis's parents were divorced. His mother had been married three times, and he had never had the security and love of a father. He really had never experienced acceptance from his mother. He felt that he never measured up to her expectations, and he was still trying to win her acceptance and his father's love, even though they were no longer living.

Dennis was a Giver. He gave and gave and gave and entertained and entertained, trying to earn, buy, and deserve approval and acceptance. He gave and entertained to win positions of influence in his church, his office, the political arena, and with friends. When he gave and entertained, there always seemed to be strings attached—a hidden agenda. He wanted recognition and to be considered when it was time to decide how the money or a gift was to be used. He did not give and turn loose of it.

When he gave to his children, there was always a price for them to pay to the point that they did not want him to give them anything. He seemed to come back later with demands, such as, "I gave you that new car. The least you can do is come over and see us on the weekend." Or he made statements like, "Looks like you could keep it clean," when he would inspect it to see if they were taking care of his gift to them.

Because Dennis's giving was so toxic, he seemed to bypass his cognitive level and give from unhealthy emotions, which made his giving erratic and unpredictable.

Sheryl was a Doer. She already had low self-esteem and insecurity about herself, their marriage, and the future. The more Dennis gave, the more critical and contemptuous Sheryl became. She complained and criticized him for his lack of maturity and his controlling of others. When he gave more and more, she felt more martyred and kept score of the "wrongs he had done to her." She also kept a subconscious checklist of the sacrifices she made because of his entertaining and giving to others.

Sheryl became more and more disillusioned with Dennis, so she threw herself into doing more and more to counterbalance the disillusionment. She kept the house immaculate, working nonstop, hand washed everything from dishes to windows, volunteered to be on all kinds of work committees, made many of their girls' clothes, cleaned the kids' rooms, and put gas in their cars for them. She was physically exhausted and angry all the time with immediate family members, and she was not sure why. But she kept going, doing, and smiling for others. She also blamed Dennis for having to work so hard, since he often invited people to their (his) home, where she felt like she was the maid.

Both Sheryl and Dennis had great potential as good marriage partners, but we had to help them see the characteristics of their very different languages. Then they could see that they were giving in to their negative, rather than their positive, characteristics. Breaking old habits is difficult for all of us, but fortunately, Dennis saw clearly that his giving and entertaining were an effort to try to

fill the void from his childhood. He was trying to buy love and acceptance. Since he was a Christian, he needed to realize that genuine
unfailing love, security, and significance can come only from God,
not from an earthly father.

Dennis was exciting to work with. As a speaker of a cognitive
language, he made an intellectual decision to get healthy and renew
his mind so that his opinion of himself lined up with God's Word and
opinion of him. He determined to stop trying to fill the void through
giving to others with the expectation of gain. His new openness and
transparency really ministered to Sheryl. She was then able to see
that she contributed to their problems, adding fuel to the flame by
judging, criticizing, working herself into exhaustion, and then acting martyred. She saw that she was developing a hardness of heart,
which was demonstrated by her disdain for clutter, laziness, disorga-
nization, emotionalism, and a lack of busyness by others. Carrying
this criticism and contempt around inside her was also showing up
in physical symptoms. She was motivated to change, get relief, and
get healthy. By doing, which is an action language, she was ready for
positive action.

Sheryl and Dennis have committed to pray over what to give
and to whom to give and when, where, and who to entertain and to
do so in agreement. Rather than stifle Dennis as he feared, this commitment has empowered him because he is now practicing the godly
principle of agreement between husband and wife. They also pray
over Sheryl's activities, which is helping her to prioritize what is
really important. We examined their issues and traced the root
causes, which brought insight and understanding. Then we began
working on their daily feelings and behavior. Sheryl and Dennis are
becoming a dynamic couple for the Lord because they are unifying
their strengths, overcoming their weaknesses, and together blessing
their family and many others through their unity.

A comment in *Modern Maturity* magazine said it well:

> **"THE WORLD IS FULL OF TWO KINDS OF PEOPLE—THE
> GIVERS AND THE TAKERS. THE TAKERS MAY EAT
> WELL, BUT THE GIVERS SLEEP WELL."**

And how true it is. Givers' hearts are light and full of the joy of sharing with others. Their lives, when under God's control, are in tune with the great Giver, the God who unselfishly gave His world the most precious gift ever given—His Son, who in turn gave His very life for us.

May we all strive to learn the beautiful behavioral language of God's Givers.

> **A WISE LOVER VALUES NOT SO MUCH THE GIFT OF THE LOVER AS THE LOVE OF THE GIVER.**
> **—*THOMAS À KEMPIS***

Kinetic Languages
The Actors

- ## The Mover
  Philippians 3:13–14

- ## The Doer
  Philippians 4:13

Speakers of kinetic languages generally respond to life, people, and values first with actions, then with their heads or hearts.

Speakers of the two kinetic (action) languages are the Mover and the Doer. These two behavioral patterns of action have many similarities, but they also have great differences.

When we think of action people, we may think of our modern-day movie and television action heroes, from G.I. Joe to Indiana Jones to James Bond to characters depicted by Clint Eastwood and Sylvester Stallone.

Other action types would likely be trailblazers, such as Davy Crockett and Daniel Boone. Many of the early pioneers who went west were probably Movers assisted by Doers, who were willing to risk their known ways of life for the adventure of the unknown.

All speakers of action languages are not superhero types, but they will invariably be active or action oriented in their approaches to life.

Mover

Direct

Assertive

Standard Bearers

*Forgetting those things
which are behind and reaching
forward to those things which
are ahead, I press toward
the goal for the prize of the
upward call of God
in Christ Jesus.*
Philippians 3:13–14

CHAPTER 9

Move It, or Lose It!

LANGUAGE 6: MOVERS

■

On a lazy Saturday afternoon, Fred was sitting on our front lawn visiting with one of our neighbors and watching the wispy summer clouds float by. They were laughing and enjoying cold soft drinks as they talked about football and other mutual interests.

Suddenly, Fred noticed a battered old van with a couple of teenagers in it turn the corner and come careening down the middle of our street. The van's windows were down, and loud rock music could be heard all the way down the block. The kids were laughing, swerving the van from side to side, and cutting up, paying little attention to their driving.

At the same instant, Fred saw our four-year-old neighbor boy, who had been playing in his yard across the street, step off the curb and into the street. Instinctively, Fred knew the van would hit the tiny boy. He jumped up and hurled his soft drink bottle at the van, making a direct hit into the windshield. The van came to a sliding, screeching stop, just barely bumping the little boy. Fred ran into the street as the shaken child got up. Although the little boy was terribly frightened, he was not hurt. Fred's quick action had saved him.

I (Anna) could tell a dozen other stories about Fred's quick actions and how they have helped people. He has rescued at least six drowning people over the years, and he does not even swim very well. He has helped police identify and arrest two rapists in the airport because he is observant and quick acting. Fred is a Mover. He is action oriented, and he is my superhero (now that I finally understand his behavioral language).

On television, the language of Movers might well apply to Murphy Brown. She is a direct, matter-of-fact, outspoken, take-charge, action-oriented, make-it-happen, get-it-done woman. She alienates and divides, but she is not ignored. Even the vice president of the United States could not ignore her. Murphy Brown *must* be addressed. She is a Mover.

PEOPLE WHOSE BEHAVIORAL LANGUAGE IS ACTION ARE FORWARD-MOVING PEOPLE. THEY ARE THE MOVERS AND SHAKERS OF THIS WORLD.

John the Baptist probably spoke this language. He was a Mover—a standard bearer who was calling others to raise their own standards. He was a visionary who spoke the truth, especially as it pertained to right and wrong.

John was results oriented. He wanted immediate repentance and response from those who heard him "crying out in the wilderness." Being open to his personal sins and faults, he was also able to see the sins and faults of others, which he was direct and frank in revealing to them.

John's boldness and persuasiveness made him a force with great impact on society. At the same time, his virtue, sincerity, and truthfulness made his message unavoidable and undeniable. His motives were pure, and his obedience to God was complete. He presented his messages with drama and flair, and there is no doubt that he won the attention of his listeners.

Dogmatic in his approach, John was uncompromising in his convictions and lacking in diplomacy, which was a contributing factor to his ultimate beheading. Yet, as a result of his dynamic ministry, multitudes followed him into the desert to hear his convicting and redeeming words. In turn, he led them to Jesus the Savior because his motives were pure, even though his manner was pushy.

Movers' Response to Life

Movers respond to life's events automatically and instinctively and then move into action. Immediately their feelings are engaged, and their action is influenced by those feelings. Their feelings are not as much about what is going on in the people around them, such as those feelings a Responder would have. Their feelings are about what is going on inside them. Their internal energy is transmitted, and their feelings energize others. Movers reflect their feelings in their facial expressions, so whether angry or happy, their feelings are seen.

While moving, their reasoning or logic kicks in. However, they often think about an action or conversation long after the event is over. If their behavior has not met their own expectations, they are quite hard on themselves. Their heart motive may have been pure, but their method may have seemed too hard, fast, or untimely. Calling upon Romans 8:28 can be quite beneficial to them.

Positive Characteristics of Movers

STRONG PERSONALITY

This person will not be ignored.

> **SOME MOVERS WILL BE LOVED, SOME MAY BE HATED, BUT NONE WILL BE IGNORED.**

Whatever they do is done with gusto and strength. Strong love, strong opinions, and strong feelings are hallmarks of the Movers' strength of personality. Their strong feelings energize them and others into action.

ACTION/RESULT ORIENTED

Proactive Movers are forward thinking. They move toward things and create results through their actions. They make things happen. Their action is not just busyness; in most cases there is accomplishment. And it is not just physical activity. Movers are in constant motion with the body, soul, and spirit. They are physically, mentally, and spiritually active and alive.

Movers can talk about and listen to ideas and plans only so long before they have to put action to them. All talk and no action frustrates them. They will usually either go into action or end the discussion out of sheer boredom. Their motto is, "Move it, or lose it!"

HIGH ENERGY

Movers can be accurately described as bundles of energy. Movers have a higher-than-average energy level, usually doing several things at a time. They seem to be in constant motion. When they sleep, it is not to rest but to recharge their batteries for tomorrow's activity. Their minds are continuously in motion, seeking creative and better ways of doing things. They are doing, feeling, talking, walking, and trying out ideas that may not be well thought out.

HONESTY

Bottom-line honesty describes Movers. Generally, there is no phoniness in their speech. They tell it like it is. Most Movers are not psychological game players or manipulators. Seldom are they good at lying or even exaggerating because their eyes, speech, and body language reveal their honest feelings and truth.

Even as little children, if given too much money as change in a store, they will return it, never thinking they could keep it. It is just not the thing to do. If other children tell lies, little Movers will be the ones who say, "No, that's a lie." Even as children, they usually call others to a higher standard of behavior.

STANDARD BEARERS

Movers' major decisions are based on convictions, not on feelings, logic, or circumstance. Their inner convictions or standards are their guiding lights. If these standards are not biblical, but are self-defined, self-serving, unrealistic, dominating, or based on some other false code, they can be problem people. However, if their standards and convictions are based on the love and understanding of God and His principles, Movers will purpose in their hearts to be pleasing to God and obedient to His standards. Movers also set high personal standards for themselves and others. They believe that aiming at high standards helps people live up to God's potential for them and to become all that they can be.

DISCERNMENT

Movers have the ability to perceive accurately the motives, character, and actions of others. Because of their high standards and strong convictions, they have a keen awareness of right and wrong, good and evil.

This discernment works when Movers deal with phoniness, manipulation, or dishonesty, as well as other expressions of an impure motive or hidden agenda. In conjunction with their high standards, their discernment may make it seem that others can never live up to their expectations. However, if you look closely, they are harder on themselves than on anyone else. They do not ask or require more of others than they require of themselves.

INTROSPECTIVE

Movers speak one of the more introspective languages. Possibly because of their desire to live by godly standards, they tend to search their hearts and souls to discover if they are operating from impure motives. They may not easily understand their deep feelings, but they willingly try to understand the purpose and motive behind their words and actions. This soul-searching creates a foundation for growth. It can also cause them to be hard on themselves when they say or do something that comes across as too harsh or judgmental, leaving them with feelings of guilt. They are fast to admit when they are wrong and, once they realize their faults, to take responsibility for them.

RISK TAKERS, VISIONARIES, AND INNOVATORS

MOVERS SEEM TO HAVE NATURAL BOLDNESS AND COURAGE TO STEP OUT, TRY SOMETHING NEW, AND CREATIVELY THINK OF NEW IDEAS AND METHODS OF DOING THINGS. THEY MAKE GOOD LEADERS.

They can work well under authority, but if there seems to be no authority or no one in charge, they will quite naturally fill the void.

Movers clearly see the vision, the end result, or the final goal. Though they can usually articulate the vision well to help others see it, they usually need help in making the detailed intermediate plans and steps of action to reach the goal. Without this assistance, they may not be able to turn the vision into a reality. Usually, that does not stop Movers. If they do not reach the first goal, they will move on toward the next goal, undaunted by the previous failure.

ASSERTIVENESS

This characteristic enables Movers to stand up for their beliefs and the rights of others, as well as express opinions openly. Assertiveness is a positive characteristic unless the pendulum swings too far and Movers become overly aggressive.

> **TRUTH WITHOUT LOVE IS AGGRESSION; LOVE WITHOUT TRUTH IS PASSIVITY; TRUTH WITH LOVE IS ASSERTIVENESS.**

It is easier for Movers to operate out of balance in aggressiveness than in passivity. This they must guard against. They are not afraid of confrontation, but the more mature they are, the less they feel that they must create confrontation.

VERBAL AND PERSUASIVE

Movers may be quite good at expressing ideas, plans, and beliefs, and because of their strength of convictions, they can be very persuasive. They are usually good conversationalists, enjoying lively discussions, sharing opinions, and debating. They can be good in sales if they believe in what they are selling because they believe *their* way is *the* way.

DRAMATIC

Many of the positive characteristics make Movers seem rather dramatic. They may say shocking things to get your attention. At times they may do something out of the ordinary to make a point. This is a result of their risk taking, courage, and innovative characteristics. This dramatic tendency also makes them memorable leaders, speakers, and teachers.

Desires of Movers

Movers are concerned about the development of inner character within others. They desire to see others move up to higher standards of inner convictions. In the spiritual realm they grieve over sin in someone's life and boldly confront the sinner, hoping to save him from destruction, bring him to repentance, and return him to a place of wholeness.

Possible Negative Characteristics of Movers

LOW SELF-ESTEEM

Because Movers are so hard on themselves when they feel that they have fallen short of their high expectations, they tend to beat up on themselves and feel guilty. They use a lot of shoulds: "I *should* have tried harder, *should* have helped more, *should* have ministered longer, *should not* have been so direct and blunt, *should* have been more patient or gentle," and on it goes.

TOO HARSH, ABRUPT, AND DIRECT

This is especially true of Movers in face-to-face interactions. Usually, Movers' *motives* are pure, but their *methods* are sometimes inappropriate—the result of doing too many things at a time and not allowing enough time for the discussion. Therefore, they may seem harsh, abrupt, or uncaring, which can lead to misunderstanding and hurt feelings. Because they are so action oriented, Movers may make a statement in passing, assuming that the listeners understand their meaning, and never intend to wound them.

Fortunately, of the speakers of all the languages, Movers are among those usually most open to reason. Movers need to slow down (or come to a complete stop) and listen. But for this to happen, their mates must confront them, call time out of all activity, announce the need to clarify some communication, and mirror back to the Movers what they heard and how they felt it was expressed. Usually, Movers are grieved that they seemed uncaring. Underneath these fast-moving people lie caring hearts.

HIGH EXPECTATIONS OF OTHERS

Movers can be hard to live with, and their mates or children may feel that they never quite measure up to the standards and expectations of Movers. Movers may realize that they project this superior image, but they probably never realize how devastating it can be to family members. Movers need to learn to show acceptance and appreciation to their children and mates. The truth is, they usually feel deep love and thankfulness for their families, but they have not taken the time to learn how to express that message.

JUDGMENTAL

Because of their ability to discern right and wrong motives, Movers may seem judgmental rather than discerning. They can easily become critical and faultfinding, trying to force people to change. The gift of discernment, which has been given to Movers, is not for the purpose of judging, forcing change, or revealing faults or weaknesses. Rather, it is for the purpose of intercession. Changing a person is the job of that individual with the help of God, not the Movers' job. Movers who use their discernment to pray and intercede for those about whom they are concerned rather than try to correct them make a powerful difference in their lives.

RESENTMENT AND BITTERNESS

If Movers have experienced a great deal of hurt and disappointment, or if they have a pattern of unresolved conflict and broken relationships, the end result will likely be resentment that leads to bitterness.

LACK OF FOLLOW-THROUGH

Movers love to start new projects, explore new horizons, embark on new ventures, and "go where no man has gone before, to seek out and search out strange new worlds." But if there is paperwork or details to handle, they will usually not get it done unless they can delegate it, and their new projects will have limited success. There is hope for the Mover who works on learning the Doer's language.

Learning self-discipline, learning to plan and follow through, is possible for Movers, but it is not easy. However, it is absolutely necessary that they either develop these abilities or hire someone who can do it for them rather than leave a trail of incompleted, disheveled projects in the wake of their all-important need to be moving. Their lifestyle reminds us of a high-speed motorboat that roars by the swimming area of a lake. They wave and smile as they zoom past and are long gone when the huge waves from their wake roll through the swimmers, splashing and dunking them.

ROLE OF THE CONSCIENCE

Because of the strength of Movers' personalities and their desire for high standards and discernment, they may try to watch and catch those who need improvement. A Mover can come across as the self-appointed commander in chief of the universe. (In years past, this was Anna's pet name for Fred.)

TENDENCY TO BE CRITICAL, CAUSTIC, AND CONTEMPTUOUS

This is the negative side of Movers' strong personalities. Without the power of the indwelling Holy Spirit, their strength often turns cruel. Movers are typically Type A personalities, and being caustic can produce fatal physical symptoms, such as heart attacks or strokes. Their very lives depend on their overcoming this tendency.

ACTING WITHOUT THINKING

Movers tend to act without first thinking through the results of the action, without appropriate planning or weighing the cost of the action. They might expose weaknesses of others without taking the time to restore their confidence and self-esteem.

PUSHY

Some Movers may be referred to as bulldozers or Mack trucks because they tend to roll over others to accomplish their own objectives. Their attitude sometimes says, "Either join me or get out of the way." Movers who learn to be careful not to crush other people in the name of getting things accomplished become some of our most influential leaders.

TENDENCY TO BLAME OTHERS

"If you had only gotten the message right, I would not have missed the appointment." Movers can easily fall into the habit of "you never" and "you always" statements. Their desire to correct others (wanting them to improve) does not motivate others to change but instead usually makes them internalize shame. Instead of their mates' hearing, "You *made* a mistake," when the Movers say it, mates tend to hear, "You *are* a mistake."

TENDENCY TO JUMP TO CONCLUSIONS

Because their minds are so active, Movers are usually ahead of you when you are talking or acting. Therefore, they tend to jump to conclusions before they have gathered all the facts. Learning to listen and wait until the data are in before concluding which action is required makes for fewer mistakes.

EXCESSIVE NEED FOR EXCITEMENT

Ungodly Movers may accelerate their level of excitement more and more until it becomes self-destructive and dangerous, both to themselves and to others. Moving is everything to them, and the faster it moves, the better they like it.

> IN THEIR DRIVING NEED TO BE MOVING, MOVERS MAY
> RUSH PAST THE GOD OF SILENCE AND STILLNESS
> WHO SOMETIMES COMES TO PEOPLE IN A WHISPER.

As Psalm 46:10 says, "Be still, and know that I am God."

PHYSICALLY ABUSIVE

Movers with negative characteristics, who have had many emotional hurts and who grew up in toxic environments, may become physically abusive. Movers naturally act physically, and they act out their feelings quickly, sometimes without thinking their actions completely through. This tendency can lead to impulsive, illogical, and wrongful behavior, such as physical abuse.

Progressive Warning Signals of Distress

This predictive model indicates or predicts the sequence Movers go through in times of normal to severe stress.

Movers signal their distress in several ways when they have not gotten their batteries charged in positive ways. Distress may cause unresolved issues to emerge and reemerge. These issues come from past hurts, toxic experiences, immaturity, stress, and lack of reliance on the Holy Spirit. The length and depth of the problems, and their failure to deal with them, determine the degree of negative distress signals. When these distress signals appear, Movers dys-

function and sabotage their personal or professional lives in predictable ways:

- First-level distress warning signals. Movers will be demanding, judgmental, and blaming. They will not give mates and
  family emotional support, expecting them to fend for themselves. They may also become overly controlling of others.
- Second-level distress warning signals. At this level of distress, Movers become resentful, caustic, and contemptuous. They may act like vengeful children and attack the
  character and person of others.
- Third-level distress warning signals. They will finally become hostile and bitter. They may pack up their personal
  belongings and move out. When third-level distress goes
  unchecked for a long period of time, Movers may become
  physically abusive. Their need for action and excitement
  may cause them to develop destructive behavior that can
  sabotage their careers (blow up at the boss) or go overboard
  on risk-taking hobbies, such as race car driving, dirt bike
  racing, or skydiving. CEOs may like to live on the edge, and
  they get a rush by making big deals that risk it all, not being
  concerned about the consequences; they may well lose it all.
  At this level, Movers may need excitement to feel alive. They
  also tend to test their mates to see if they will abandon them
  and leave their marriages when times get tough.

How Do I Love Thee?

ACTION AND APPROVAL

Movers feel loved when their mates share action deeds or activities with and for them.

**MOVERS NEED TO FEEL THEIR MATES' APPROVAL, NOT
SO MUCH FOR WHAT THEY HAVE DONE, BUT FOR WHO
THEY ARE: SPECIAL, LOVED, SIGNIFICANT, PRECIOUS
CHILDREN OF GOD.**

For Movers to feel loved, your words and beliefs must line up
with your actions. They need to see congruency in their mates' lives,

that you are honest in how you relate to them. This causes the Mover to be secure in your love and to trust you.

If you are married to a Mover, it is important to be honest.

> **TO MOVERS, HONESTY = TRUST = SECURITY = LOVE. OR HONESTY CREATES TRUST, WHICH RESULTS IN SECURITY AND PRODUCES CONFIDENCE THAT THEY ARE LOVED.**

Although this works with all languages, it is of utmost importance to Movers because of their high standards and built-in personal honesty.

Although Movers primarily speak an action language and feel loved when others *do* things for them, they will continually look for the motive behind the action. In other words, if I cook breakfast for Fred because he will get mad at me if I don't, and I do it out of a sense of duty or resentment, it will not be very meaningful to him. But if I do it as an expression of my love for him, he feels loved. Movers will know your real motive, even if you try to hide it from them.

If a man washes his wife's car and then uses it to take his buddies to a ball game, his Mover wife will question his motives. She will think, *He didn't do this because he loves me; he did it for himself.* If the husband then tries to convince his Mover wife, "Hey, I did this because I love you," the wife will focus on the incongruity and probably reject the action. If the husband is not in touch with his motives, he will probably be confused, walk off shaking his head, and say, "Nothing I do seems to please that woman."

Movers are quick to spot self-serving words and actions. Once trust begins to erode because of past deceptions, Movers will question actions that might serve as cover-ups for deceptive behaviors. They are prone to suspicion and jealousy.

For a Mover to feel loved, your motives must be pure. Then the Mover will feel loved when you clean the house, paint the porch, or wash the car because you are saying, "This well-cared-for home is an expression of my love for you. I really love you!"

Because Movers find manipulation and exaggeration distasteful, mates need to speak truth without a lot of fluff or embellishment.

Movers are bottom-line people. So, when you relate a story or incident, the Mover likes to hear the ending first, then you can go back and fill in the details. Do not start a long story and build the suspense through lots of detail, waiting till the last minute before you say whether the car was totaled or not. It is best to start with, "I really had quite an experience today. I nearly wrecked the car, but fortunately, I did not. Let me tell you what happened."

To show your love, ask your action-oriented mate what you can do for him or her today. What can you do to help? Remember that a Mover needs excitement and action in life, so the mate who joins in and keeps life exciting will make the Mover feel loved.

SPIRITUAL MOTIVATION

Each of the seven behavioral languages correlates to one of the motivational gifts listed in Romans 12:5–8. The Mover's behavioral style generally correlates to the spiritual gift of prophecy. Each gift of grace is vital to the health and growth of the church, the body of Christ. Movers call us forward, ever forward, in our focus and action for the Lord.

FINANCIAL STYLE

Honesty is the bottom line to Movers and their money. However, due to their risk-taking characteristics and their sometimes acting before they have gathered all the facts, they may tend to invest or spend rather flamboyantly. Later their action may prove to have been unwise. Because they act, then think, they may spend, then regret. If they will be patient, they have the ability to make wonderfully wise investments because of their discernment and desire for honesty. However, if they do make unwise decisions or investments, they will quickly see their error, get out as soon as possible, and move on to something new.

Movers are not naturally good day-to-day money managers because they do not take time to follow through on the details. So, this may be an area that is best delegated to someone else, such as an accountant or a mate who is good at details and day-to-day money management. Movers like to be involved, consulted, or allowed to be overseers, but let someone else do the daily matters and keep the checkbook in balance.

Movers like to buy; they just do not like to shop or look. They have little patience with shopping, but if they have specific shopping missions, such as buying a blouse or hammer, they can accomplish their missions and enjoy the outings. Window-shopping, though, is nothing more than a waste of valuable time to them because it accomplishes nothing concrete.

ENTERTAINMENT STYLE

Movers are usually at ease in large or small crowds, but when they have a choice, they often prefer smaller groups with a few good friends. They like stimulating, lively conversation and discussions, but they also like activities. Movers like to cook outside, go to the park, play tennis, plan picnics, and share days at the lake or zoo, just as long as either the conversation or the activity keeps moving.

Movers enjoy entertaining people in their homes, and they tend to make people feel welcome and comfortable.

THE HOME

Movers' homes are very important to them. They (like Doers) want their homes to be functional and serviceable. Yet, because of their risk-taking and dramatic flair, their homes are generally not as practical as Doers' homes. They are not status quo people; they are usually open to expanding, remodeling, redecorating, and improving. Or they may enjoy the fun of selling one house and moving to another. Movers always look for ways to improve their environments.

Because the Movers' outside world may be a place of conflict, strong opinions, fast action, accomplishment, and activities, their homes need to be places of peace, sanctuary, refuge, nurturing, and rebuilding. They generally like thick carpets, overstuffed chairs, and any gadgets or electronic equipment that can bring excitement or comfort into their lives. They like game rooms, yards, patios, and pools that allow for movement and activities.

MOVERS AND SEX

Movers can be exciting lovers because they tend to act, then feel. With their activated feelings they are very comfortable in giving and receiving sexual love. Because marital sex involves so much more than what goes on in the bedroom, Movers need to receive approval for who they are from their mates throughout the day, to know that they are special, significant, and loved. This approval gives them security to help them overcome their tendency to be hard on themselves and have low self-esteem, even about their lovemaking. Movers need to acknowledge this characteristic and take personal responsibility, and not put excessive expectations on their mates to meet all their needs. Movers can flourish into sensitive, caring, committed mates and lovers. They like change, excitement, and romance.

Movers typically resist sexual temptations because of their strong convictions and sense of right and wrong. They place great importance on commitment, which gives them built-in protection from relationships outside marriage. However, if they are not protected by strong biblical convictions, Movers can get involved before they realize it since they act, feel, and later think. They later suffer great remorse and guilt, even if all they do is entertain the idea of giving in to the sexual temptation. Movers would probably confess the extramarital affair to their mates and ask for forgiveness. Movers may withhold sex as a form of punishment, but it would be difficult for them to do this long.

Last-Ditch Hope

Fran and Steve came to us for counseling as a last-ditch hope for their marriage and family. The outward appearances indicated that they were destroying each other and their children. Their Christian friends and family had already given up on them, feeling that their hurts, disappointments, and bitterness were too deep.

Fran tested out to be a strong Mover; Steve was a Responder. He saw her as a dominating, hard, unloving wife. She saw him as a passive, weak, irresponsible husband. Fran had moved into second-level distress and was staying there most of the time. She was angry, resentful, and contemptuous. She demanded that Steve be more exciting, decisive, and strong, and since he was not displaying those characteristics, she blamed him for all her unhappiness.

Their three children were acting out the insecurities of the parents' rocky marriage by open rebellion, depression, withdrawal, overachieving, and anorexia. Was there hope for this marriage and family?

After testing their languages, we asked them to make a contract with us that they would make no major decisions or changes, such as separating or filing for divorce, for an agreed period of time. Then we began working with Fran and Steve in both individual and joint counseling. Gradually, they began to see each other as individuals and as a couple in a new light. They started catching the vision of how each strength balanced the other's weaknesses. And by building on and appreciating the positive characteristics of each other, and seeing each as God's gift to the other, they began to change, grow, and heal.

Steve and Fran had deep hurts, broken trust, and destructive habits. They started learning to express their feelings rather than withdraw or fight unfairly. And they found new tools to work with through insight and understanding of each other's language. They learned to say "I love you" in the language that each needed to hear. In other words, they became bilingual. As each learned the language to use to meet the other's needs, they stopped demanding that their own needs be met.

Each difference of opinion did not have to be a showdown or a fight to the finish for Fran. They both started learning tolerance and forgiveness.

Did the children's problems immediately go away? No, but through testing each child and learning his or her language, and through continuing family therapy, they are learning to communicate as a family and to love in healthier ways.

The teenager in rebellion is getting in touch with his fears and realizing he does not have to act tough to cover them up. He speaks the same language as his mother; he is a Mover. He and his mother are exploring their primary language together.

The depressed, withdrawn son is learning that he does not have to hide his insecurities and anger by turning those feelings inward on himself out of fear of rejection. His second language is Responder, the same as his father's, and his primary language is Contemplator. He is now spending quality time with his father doing things that will bond them in their common language, and together they are exploring his primary language, Contemplator.

The overachieving anorexic daughter is learning that she does not have to be perfect to be loved and appreciated, and that she does not have to hold on to the anorexia to be in control of at least one area of her life. She is a Strategist, and the family is learning how to help her develop that special language. She plans, schedules, and assigns roles and duties to each family member to discuss or act out so that all family members are learning all seven languages. They spend one hour weekly doing this as a family. The daughter is in charge of the weekly meeting and the agreed-upon activities and events that come out of that meeting. She then delegates responsibility to each family member based on consensus, the family mission statement, and individual mission statements they now use to stay focused.

Fran and Steve are finally allowing their children to be children and each other to be human. They are still working on their issues, but in a year's time they have gone from a disastrous marriage and a destructive family system to a committed marriage and a supportive family, working together, learning to appreciate one another, with a realistic hope for the future. Understanding differences brings acceptance and appreciation of uniqueness. Becoming multilingual is a loving and logical way to begin.

On the Move

Mary's (our coauthor's) parents have moved forty-seven times during their fifty-seven-year marriage. In fact, they moved in and out of the same house on Caddo Street in Greenville, Texas, three different times! Each time they moved into that house, they had the same two men from Wolf Moving Company in Greenville to help them. Mary says, "Those guys were like part of the family. We didn't even have to tell them where the furniture went in the house—they already knew. They even knew that the upright piano we had bought between moves was new."

Mary also says, "We moved so much through the years that my mom used to laugh and say that every time the television accidentally got unplugged, it ran out on the porch and waited to be loaded. And when I was away at college, my mom would draw a diagram of whatever different house they were moving to and mail it to me so I would know where my room was when I came home."

> SOME PEOPLE JUST HAVE TO BE ON THE MOVE. THEY
> ARE CALLED FORWARD BY WHAT THEY SEE AS
> POSSIBILITIES IN THE FUTURE. THEIR PROPHETIC
> GIFT FROM GOD PULLS THEM OUT OF THE PAST, AND
> EVEN THE PRESENT, TO VISTAS "OUT THERE
> SOMEWHERE."

They are the beautiful people who keep us from resting on our past accomplishments or failures and lead us forward with excitement and enthusiasm. God bless the Movers as they bless us!

> THE BEST COMPLIMENT WE CAN PAY OUR PAST IS TO
> PROPHETICALLY AND BRAVELY FACE TODAY AND
> TOMORROW.
> —*BERNIE WIEBE*

Doer

Dedicated

Observant

Conscientious

*I can do all things through
Christ who strengthens me.*
Philippians 4:13

CHAPTER 10

Doing—What Comes Naturally

LANGUAGE 7: DOERS

■

Years ago General William Booth, leader of the Salvation Army, was losing his eyesight, and his assistants announced that his days of usefulness were, regrettably, over. The General remained in seclusion for several weeks while one eye was surgically removed and he slowly recovered.

At long last General Booth appeared once again in public, with only very limited sight in his remaining eye. To a spellbound audience of over four thousand people in London he spoke for over an hour and a half. Here is what this almost-blind servant of God said: "I want to do more for humanity, and I want to do a great deal more for Jesus. There are thousands of poor, wretched, suffering, and sinning people crying out to us for help, and I want to do something for them."

General Booth was, no doubt, a Doer. He wanted to do even more than he had done in his busy forty years of concentrated service. He could not live with the thought of doing nothing. Even with debilitating blindness, he could think only of doing something worthwhile for others.

The philosopher John Dewey once found his son in the bathroom where the floor was flooded. The professor began thinking, trying to understand the situation, how it had occurred, and what to do about it. After working a few minutes alone, the son said to his analytically immobilized father, "Dad, this is not the time to philosophize. This is the time to mop!"

That is a Doer's answer to everything. Get busy. *Do* something. A Doer believes the old adage that says, "The smallest deed is better than the greatest intention." And

---

IT WAS PROBABLY A DOER WHO FIRST SAID, "LEAD, FOLLOW, OR GET OUT OF THE WAY. *DO* SOMETHING!"

In the Bible, a great example of a Doer is Moses. Doers love to meet others' needs by doing things for them, especially doing with their hands. God knew Moses was a Doer, so He spoke to Moses in his primary behavioral language, saying, "Let's start with what is in your hand, or what is at hand" (Exod. 4:2). He gave Moses many ways to be a Doer or to use his hand. He told Moses to put forth his hands, to put his hand on his bosom, and to stretch his hand out. Moses was a hands-on doing leader.

Exodus 4:10 is the classic Moses-the-Doer verse. Doers may be quite verbal, but usually, they do not like to speak in public. Moses said, "O my Lord, I am not eloquent, neither before nor since You have spoken to Your servant; but I am slow of speech and slow of tongue." He was saying, let me help someone, let me do something, but choose another as spokesman for Your people. He did not have the confidence that he could lead, motivate, and articulate.

God knew Moses was really right. So, even though He insisted that Moses be the leader, He gave Moses an assistant, Aaron, to speak for him, acting as a mouthpiece for God. Moses went about doing all the other tasks of leadership—happily. Moses knew innately that doing was his communication style, while Aaron may have been an Influencer.

A take-charge leader such as a Mover would have become so impatient with the Israelites he probably would have said, "You guys can stay here grumbling if you want to, but I'm out of here." And he would have gone on without them—after only a week or two. A natural leader such as a Strategist would have immediately made an overall plan to get them to the Promised Land, including people, jobs, and equipment. The Strategist would have made a map, organized a food committee, found moving vehicles, set up a packing committee, and appointed a shelter-tent committee. The Strategist would have had them in Israel in about two weeks, but that was not God's plan. He knew they needed to spend time in the wilderness to develop their character and to remove the influence of the Egyptian culture from them. That took time. So He gave them Moses, the Doer.

The Israelites grumbled and complained about everything Moses did. He was not able to motivate them, as an Influencer might have done. He did not like to speak in public; he probably did not have a charismatic personality; so it was hard for the Israelites to hold on to the vision of the Promised Land. They kept wanting to go back into Egypt, even into slavery.

Moses was always busy, active, working, moving, and energetic. But poor Moses had major trouble keeping God's people focused, motivated, united, and directed toward their goal and vision.

God's choice of a reluctant leader was not a mistake. Moses fulfilled God's plan perfectly in the long run. It was all according to God's time schedule, and no speaker of another language could have led in a way to fulfill that nearly as well as Moses did. The Bible tells us that God loved Moses so much that He personally buried him in a valley of the land of Moab because of all the great and mighty deeds that Moses wrought in the sight of all Israel (Deut. 34:5–12).

What honor God bestowed on Moses the Doer! God rewards the faithful.

Possibly the most obvious Doer in the Bible is Martha, the special friend at whose house Jesus often ate and stayed. Martha was always busy. On one occasion she was whipping up a large dinner. Her sister, Mary (possibly a Responder), was letting her do it while Mary sat in the living room visiting with their friends. Martha is the one who got things done and upon whom everyone else obviously depended.

PRAISE THE LORD FOR DOERS, ELSE WE MIGHT ALL STARVE!

Fred's father, Frank, is an example of a Doer. He was one of the most practical, pragmatic persons you could ever hope to meet. He was action oriented, but rather than make things happen, he responded to needs around him. He was the man the whole community called on for any problem, whether it was sickness, finance, politics, or a family crisis. He was always there for everyone.

Frank was always ready for an emergency. He operated the ambulance service and volunteer fire department and housed them on his property, and he was a deputy sheriff of the county.

Doers are responsible people, and Frank fit that mold perfectly. He was a member of the school board for 35 years and was its president for 25 years. He was a reluctant leader. Frank would have preferred supporting someone else in that position, but because the community felt he was the most qualified person for the job, they kept reelecting him.

Doers are excellent maintainers and are happy in the same job for long periods of time. Frank had the same retail business for over 50 years—a combination garage, filling station, hardware store, and more. Always ready to serve the needs of the community and the ranchers, he spent his life working with his hands, doing detail work, serving, and being useful. His business was organized and orderly. No matter how many suggestions his wife or Fred or others made that he expand and hire an assistant, Frank would not do it. It was more trouble for him to delegate and train than to do it himself.

Frank was not especially introspective. He had little patience and tolerance for people who tried to analyze the "why" of things—the motives behind the actions. His philosophy was, "If it needs doing, then do it," and, "If it's broken, fix it."

He had a practical view of God: if it was in the Word, just believe it. God was in charge, and that was all there was to that. Faith was as natural to him as breathing, and he didn't understand those who agonized about obedience. To Frank, obedience brought blessings, and disobedience just didn't work.

At the same time Frank and his wife moved onto their property, they donated the land on which the Tinnie Baptist Church was built. They founded the church, and it is still open today. (They also donated the land on which the grade school was built—when Doers give, it is for practical purposes.) For several years the church wanted Frank to be a deacon, but he wouldn't do it. Consistently and generously serving and helping, Frank never accepted the position of deacon because he didn't feel qualified, yet he supported the church faithfully with his tithes and offerings, took in visiting missionaries, and seldom missed a service.

He lived on the same property for 56 years, although he did move from one house into another one—a lovely, two-story, 200-year-old adobe house—after he and his wife restored it.

Frank's life was an example to all, and he was a role model of a humble man of faith—a man who loved his family, served his community, and showed his love by being dependable and responsible.

Doers' Response to Life

When Doers respond to life events, they first "start the action." Many times this is before gathering all the facts needed to make quality decisions. They "see a need and want to meet it." To them whatever needs to be done is obvious and usually practical, and they are programmed to respond. Even if sometimes their action proves to have been too quick or even turns out to be a mistake, their law of averages causes them to still get more accomplished than the persons of other languages who are slower to act.

Doers act—then they think about it maybe halfway through, and then last of all they feel. Their action is rapid and their thinking is more instinctive than deliberate or a thorough reasoning process. Their feelings—although they do feel deeply—are not easily accessed and may not be a conscious consideration in their decision-making.

Positive Characteristics of Doers

ACTION ORIENTED

Doers like to stay busy, especially with hands-on projects, from landscaping, flower arranging, or woodworking to setting up the chairs or cleaning up after a meeting. They are not physically lazy and have little tolerance for people who are. Doers go into action as soon as they are aware of a need. Their action usually revolves around seeing a need and filling it, whether it is a personal, family, community, church, or corporate need. Doers are usually ready, willing, and able to do what is required to meet needs.

REACTORS

> **WHERE MOVERS *MAKE* THINGS HAPPEN, DOERS *REACT* (IN A POSITIVE WAY) TO THINGS THAT ARE ALREADY HAPPENING. THEY RESPOND TO NEEDS AROUND THEM AND DO SOMETHING ABOUT THEM.**

If they see hungry children, they feed them. If they find a closet that needs straightening, they do it. If they hear a cry for assistance, they help. Whatever their eyes see to do, their hands and feet respond to accomplish.

PRAGMATIC

Doers' thinking and actions emphasize practicality. They react to life, challenges, or problems from a practical perspective. They see and are comfortable meeting practical needs. Doers are practical in thought, word, and deed.

DESIRE TO BE USEFUL

Doers love to know that they have been helpful to someone. They have a great desire to be of real service. They are extremely valuable when it comes to getting projects finished; they are the cogs in the wheels of progress.

AWARENESS OF IMMEDIATE NEEDS AND SHORT-RANGE GOALS

Rather than focus on the overall big picture and long-range goals, Doers are do-it-now people. Later will take care of itself. Do not put Doers in charge of next year's family reunion. Put them in charge of this week's luncheon, and they will succeed. (Put Strategists in charge of next year's reunion.)

GOOD AT DETAIL WORK AND KEEPING SCHEDULES

Doers have certain days for doing certain jobs. They love "to do" lists, shopping lists, and schedules. Their calendars are accurate and up-to-date. They have a good memory for details.

HIGH ENERGY

Doers are not prone to pace themselves, do not feel that they need to take rest breaks, and hate being idle. People of this language stay busy, whether much is being accomplished or not. You will not find them sitting for hours in front of the television unless they are doing some project with their hands while they watch.

NOT TOO INTROSPECTIVE

This trait is part of Doers' practical makeup. If it needs to be done, just do it, and do not try to figure out why. This trait causes them to be less in touch with their feelings or the feelings of others.

GOOD VERBAL SKILLS

Doers prefer action with talk or action without talk, yet they are typically good communicators. To them, it is a waste of time to talk for hours, or even minutes, about a problem when the solution is plain and action is required. Their answer to problems is action, not analysis. To them, it is always "time to mop."

AVOIDANCE OF THE SPOTLIGHT

Doers would rather be support people. Although they may have good verbal skills, they prefer not to speak in public or to be on the stage. They would rather work behind the scenes getting things done, taking care of details so that things run smoothly and efficiently. They play second fiddle with a real flair. However, if it is thrust upon them, they will rise to the occasion. They protest recognition but do enjoy and need proper recognition.

RELUCTANCE TO SAY NO

Since doing is *the* thing to them, saying no to opportunities to do or serve is next to impossible. That is why Doers often get overextended and may not take good care of themselves or their families.

METICULOUS

Doers have a place for everything and want everything in its place. They like their shirts ironed a certain way, lined up in an orderly fashion, possibly even color-coded to match certain suits. Doers organize their garages, labeling everything. They have their kitchens in perfect order, with their shelves labeled. People of other languages can do this from time to time, but Doers keep things this way. They maintain the tidy organization. They may be the people we refer to as neatniks.

DESIRES OF DOERS

The Doer desires to meet the practical, pragmatic, functional, and physical needs of others through helping and serving. These diligent servants keep our world turning.

Possible Negative Characteristics of Doers

LOW SELF-ESTEEM

Doers are often uncomfortable when others do things for them or serve them. Doers may struggle with feelings of unworthiness.

> **DOERS BELIEVE THAT THEIR WORTH COMES FROM *DOING* RATHER THAN *BEING*. THEY TEND TO SEE THEMSELVES AND OTHERS MORE AS "HUMAN DOINGS" THAN AS "HUMAN BEINGS."**

A mate of a Doer can help overcome this sense of unworthiness by offering reinforcement. You might say, "Although I appreciate all that you *do*, I really love and value you for *who you are*. You are special, and I love you." However, this reinforcement must be sincere and ongoing for a lifetime. Because the tendency of low self-esteem is well ingrained, a Doer needs to hear over and over, "I appreciate what you do, but I love who you are."

As far as being served by a mate, a Doer will probably always struggle with it, but deep down it makes him or her feel special. So, do things for your Doer mate, who may have to learn to become a good receiver over a lifetime of your love and care.

CRITICAL AND CONTEMPTUOUS

Doers tend to see others who are not practical and action oriented as having something wrong with them. And their intolerance of emotional situations and people may cause them to be critical of others. This criticism, if unchecked, can become judgment, develop into contemptuousness, and even lead to bitterness.

Mates of Doers need to remember that criticism is not about who *you* are but about who *they* are. Becoming nondefensive about this characteristic and working on overcoming it, allowing their mates to be a part of helping, can open up new areas of understanding and communication for Doers. As the scripture says, "Keep your heart with all diligence, for out of it spring the issues of life" (Prov. 4:23).

MARTYRED

When Doers do not receive praise and appreciation for all the hard work and effort they have put into something, they may feel martyred. They also feel martyred if they think they are the only ones doing the work. They want everyone to be like them, to be Doers, too.

TENDENCY TO KEEP SCORE

Doers are different from Responders, who keep score of hurts and wrongs done to them. Doers keep score of what they have done in comparison to what others have done or haven't done. "I did this and this and this, and you did not do anything," or, "I'm the only one who ever does anything around here." This feeds their tendency to feel martyred and become critical of others.

TRYING TO FILL AN INAPPROPRIATE NEED

Doers sometimes respond immediately to a need and do not always check with higher authorities to see if there is another plan perhaps already in motion to fill the need. For instance, Doers may see that the carpet of the church needs to be cleaned. They check it again Wednesday night, and when it is not done, they rent a carpet cleaner on Thursday and clean it themselves. Later they learn that the carpet was replaced the following Monday morning. So, instead of receiving praise for a job well done, they find others are irritated that they acted without checking with authorities and spent money and time unnecessarily.

IMPATIENT

Doers want to do it *now*. They start a job and finish it as soon as possible because they are motivated by short-range goals. When getting the job done takes a bit too long, it brings on their impatience, both with themselves and with others. Doers who are writers, for instance, may stick to short stories or children's picture books rather than epic novels.

OVERLY SENSITIVE

> **ALTHOUGH DOERS MAY BE CRITICAL OF OTHERS, THEY HAVE DIFFICULTY RECEIVING CRITICISM. ANY CRITICISM OF WHAT THEY DO STRIKES AT THE VERY HEART OF WHO THEY ARE AND PUTS PAINFUL DENTS IN THEIR SELF-ESTEEM.**

NEGLECTFUL OF NEEDS OF SELF AND FAMILY

Because doing is the key to their self-image, Doers have difficulty saying no to requests or needs of others. Overextending themselves then causes them to experience burnout. Taking food to people who are sick, leading the men's group, sponsoring the Cub Scouts, helping a neighbor build a deck, and working at the office over the weekend all add up to emotional and physical fatigue for Doers.

MISUNDERSTOOD SPIRITUAL NATURE

We have a friend who was an administrative assistant for a large Christian organization. He was concerned about the practical needs of the organization, such as getting the buildings painted, keeping the landscaping maintained, making sure that the floors and windows were clean, and seeing that the money that he was budgeted was managed well and met as many of the needs as possible.

Many of the other staff members considered him not very spiritual. In group prayer, for instance, he might be praying with his eyes open, noticing some of the practical needs around him and making a mental note to take care of them. It was not that he was necessarily less spiritual; he was just operating in the behavioral language that God had given him. If the other staff members had learned to recognize his behavioral language instead of criticizing him, they would have appreciated his uniqueness and his meeting needs that they were unaware of and would not have wanted to be bothered with anyway.

PERCEPTION OF EMOTIONS AS A SIGN OF WEAKNESS

Because of their focus on meeting practical needs, Doers often miss the emotional needs of others. When they do become aware of them, unless the emotional people can get over the pain, hurt, or depression right away, Doers tend to lose patience with them. Doers' attitude is usually, "If you would just get up and do something, you would feel better and not be as depressed. Get on with life." This tendency often causes them to deny their feelings, and they may have difficulty sharing, expressing, and owning their emotional sides.

> **DO NOT EXPECT DOERS TO BARE THEIR SOULS TO YOU; IT IS NOT THEIR NATURE. THIS DOES NOT MEAN THAT THEY HAVE NO EMOTIONS, ONLY THAT THEY DO NOT OFTEN EXPRESS THEM TO OTHERS.**

EASILY HURT WHEN OTHERS DO NOT SHOW APPRECIATION

Doers' self-esteem is built on appreciation for what they do. They may internalize a lack of appreciative expression as a lack of approval on your part; thus, they suffer self-image bruises.

HARD TIME DELEGATING OR TURNING LOOSE

Even if mates or family members have more time, or they are better equipped to do the job, Doers will tend to continue trying to do it all themselves rather than turning loose. In the business world this trait can really be a limitation. Also in the home, it can prevent unity and a sense of shared purpose.

TENDENCY TO BLAME OTHERS

Doers are reluctant to take responsibility for their faults, failures, or mistakes. Since failures and mistakes are usually connected to doing, and doing is at the very core of their self-image, denying their faults or shifting the blame is Doers' way of protecting themselves and falsely retaining their self-respect.

Progressive Warning Signals of Distress

This predictive model indicates or predicts the sequence Doers go through in times of normal to severe stress.

Doers signal their distress in several ways when they have not gotten their batteries charged in positive ways. Distress may cause unresolved issues to emerge and reemerge. These issues come from past hurts, toxic experiences, immaturity, stress, and lack of reliance on the Holy Spirit. The length and depth of the problems, and their failure to deal with them, determine the degree of negative distress signals. When these distress signals appear, Doers dysfunction and sabotage their personal or professional lives in predictable ways:

- First-level distress warning signals. Doers expect perfection of self and others. They blame and become judgmental at this level of distress.
- Second-level distress warning signals. They may begin to lecture and preach and become critical or caustic. They may move into martyrdom and unforgiveness. They brood and become resentful.
- Third-level distress warning signals. Doers may develop depression, bitterness, and self-pity. Their anger may be expressed through contempt as well as through accusing and rejecting others. Their anger finally turns to alienation, then to verbal or physical abuse.

How Do I Love Thee?

APPROVAL

Doers need your approval. To let Doers know that they are loved is a rather uncomplicated procedure. Just do things for them and with them. Or just *do* things; be active! Cook their meals; organize their closets; mow the yard; go to work. They see all these actions as expressions of your love. If you did not love them, you would not do these actions. The Doer husband or wife says, "Of course I love you. I work every day, maintain this house, and take care of my family. That's how I let you know that you are loved." Doers may not remember to buy gifts or to actually say "I love you" very often, but they feel that they show the depth of their love by the things they do for you.

Do they also need verbal reinforcement? You bet. Doers need to hear words of appreciation. They need to know that you take notice of all their work and efforts. Praise them often, in many ways, and mention it to others. That makes them feel that you truly appreciate them for what they *do* and so for who they *are*.

They may say, "Oh, it was really nothing," but they want and have a real need to know that you notice their deeds. Praise is as necessary as food for the good emotional and social health of these special people. Without it, they feel unappreciated and martyred.

So, let your Doer mate know how much you appreciate all that is done and how valuable he or she is to you.

Doers want their mates to have projects, too. They do not like for their mates and families to just sit around and talk. As a matter of fact, they have difficulty understanding how people can do that or how people can talk on the phone so long. Doers will state their business quickly and get off the phone to get busy again. They expect mates to be busy, also. It is all right for mates to help them with the projects they are doing, but they do not like to delegate, instruct, or teach others how to do a job. They would rather do it themselves than take the time to teach or delegate. They are generally not good developers of people. They may apprentice others, but the apprentices must make it their decision to watch and learn.

SPIRITUAL MOTIVATION

Each of the seven behavioral languages correlates to one of the motivational gifts listed in Romans 12:5–8. The Doer's behavioral style generally correlates to the spiritual gift of ministry or serving. Each gift of grace is vital to the health and growth of the church, the body of Christ. Doers are beautiful examples of service, who teach us to minister humbly to one another.

FINANCIAL STYLE

Consistent with their pragmatic personalities, Doers are not extravagant. They usually do not buy things on the spur of the moment, nor are they prone to buy things that are not practical and useful. However, they will use their finances to meet the practical needs of others. And because of their impatience in following the normal channels or waiting for someone else to do it, they may seem impetuous, jump in, and buy something to get the job done. Sometimes they find out that the money was well spent, appreciated, and helpful. Other times they may find out it was not called for.

A Doer friend of ours was frustrated because the company she worked for would not provide the software that her office needed to complete a project. She called around and found the best price. The software was not that expensive, so if the company would not reimburse her, she would not be out that much. At least she could get the job done and could stop wasting time. Fortunately, the situation worked out the way she had hoped it would. She got the job done, and her boss appreciated it and reimbursed her for the software. However, had the expense been much greater, her boss might not have done so, as the company was in the process of upgrading all computers and installing new programs. At that time the software she purchased would have been ineffective. Doers take action like that, and it does not always work out.

Doers are not extravagant in spending money on themselves or their families. Their investments are generally practical, consistent, low risk, and safe. And they tend to be diligent providers and good money managers.

ENTERTAINMENT STYLE

When entertaining, although Doers make people feel welcome in their homes, they do not share the gift of hospitality that Givers have. When Doers serve a meal, it is good, basic, and nutritional, but it may not be especially fancy or lavish. They tend to be more practical, meat-and-potatoes cooks. People generally feel comfortable in their homes, but Doers do not go out of their way to make others feel like royalty.

Doers have many friends because they serve so many people. However, they have difficulty feeling intimate and being emotionally transparent with people. They are comfortable with and enjoy both small and large groups.

They generally like entertaining that has some activity, such as picnics, barbeques, swimming parties, and more.

THE HOME

Doers want their homes to be practical, functional, serviceable, easy to keep clean, neat, and orderly. They are usually not extravagant or dramatic in their decor and design. They seldom, if ever, rearrange the furniture. (That is because they decided where the most functional, logical place for it was to begin with, so why move it?) They do not have lots of knickknacks or art objects sitting around because they see them as clutter. Although Doers may travel a great deal, they have few mementos from their trips. To them, silk flowers take a lot of time to dust, and many houseplants take time to water and tend. They usually have nice yards with lovely plants but not necessarily the kind that require constant pruning. Their bookshelves will probably be topically arranged, books graduating in height and all standing upright with nothing else on the shelves. Many times they like traditional furniture and furniture that is handcrafted because of the quality of the work and the fact that it will last for generations.

DOERS AND SEX

Doers are not by nature prone to romantic settings or romantic words and music. To them, sex is a practical need, although pleasurable and important. They certainly do not mind if the mood is romantic, but they would probably not think to set that mood themselves, and it would not be especially needed. So the Doer, if married to someone who wants more romance, must learn to incorporate romance into intimate moments. Doers must realize that if it is important to their mates, they should make an effort to be romantic.

Mates of Doers need to realize that lack of romance, originality, and flair in their intimate moments and sexual activities does *not* mean lack of love, interest, or pleasure. If it is important to you, be open and express that need, but do it in a practical, nonemotional, or nonaccusatory way. Doers do not respond well to emotional outbursts. Once they understand the benefits of strengthening the sexual intimacy, they will respond to that need.

Nothing Doing

When Joe and Martha attended one of our seminars on the behavioral languages, they rushed up after the first session and said perhaps this teaching could help them. If not, they were ready to throw in the towel. Although they loved each other, they were so frustrated and so angry that Martha's physical health was affected and Joe admitted that he feared he was becoming impotent. They had decided that maybe if they separated for a while, cooled off, and stopped being so upset, they could see whether things were fixable.

They were attending a three-day seminar; Joe and Martha were faithful to attend each session. They did their homework, participated in the small-group interaction, and seemed serious about wanting their marriage to be helped and healed.

We set up an appointment to meet with them for a couple of hours before we had to catch our plane. They discovered their languages. Martha is a Doer, with strong perfectionistic tendencies, making unrealistic demands on herself and family, and constantly overextending herself with too many involvements outside the home. Joe is a Contemplator, who likes to guard his time, and he felt that Martha, the children, and all her projects and commitments were constantly invading his time and space. He was stressed out; he felt unloved and unimportant.

In other words, Martha was trying to show her love for Joe by *doing things* for him, but Joe understood love as her *doing nothing* with him. The flip side was also true: to Martha, Joe's love for her was evidenced by what he was busy *doing* for her. So, the more he *did nothing*, the more unloved she felt. (A Contemplator will put everything aside and close all other people and activities out to spend uninterrupted, quality time with his mate. Doers see this as doing nothing.) As each one struggled harder to experience love in his or her own special way, they pulled farther and farther apart— one *doing things*, the other *doing nothing*.

Joe and Martha stayed in touch with us and had several telephone counseling appointments. They practically memorized the teaching tapes on the behavioral languages. The really exciting thing is that the Lord did more than restore their marriage. As they began to understand each other's needs for love, Martha began doing fewer things, and Joe began doing more things. Their relationship immediately began to grow together rather than apart. They started a Bible study group in their home based on this concept, and the last time we heard, almost two dozen marriages had been saved and strengthened through their instruction on the languages and their personal example and transparency.

Second Fiddle

A famous conductor of a great symphony orchestra was asked which instrument he considered the most difficult to play. The conductor thought for a moment, then said, "Second fiddle. I can get plenty of first violinists. But finding someone who can play second fiddle with enthusiasm—that's a problem. And if we have no second fiddles, we have no harmony!"

DOERS ARE THE REACTORS TO LIFE. THEY PROVIDE HARMONY TO THE SOUNDS OF LIFE. THEY PLAY SECOND FIDDLE WITH A FLAIR. AND THEY ARE JUST *DOING*—IT'S WHAT COMES NATURALLY.

ACTION MAY NOT ALWAYS BRING HAPPINESS; BUT THERE IS NO HAPPINESS WITHOUT ACTION.
—*BENJAMIN DISRAELI*

PART THREE

Putting the Languages to Work for Your Marriage

■

I WOULD MUCH
RATHER SPEAK FIVE
WORDS THAT
PEOPLE CAN
UNDERSTAND AND
BE HELPED BY,
THAN TEN
THOUSAND WORDS
. . . IN AN
UNKNOWN
LANGUAGE.

■

1 CORINTHIANS 14:19 TLB

CHAPTER 11

Your Marriage Investment Portfolio

A LOVE INVESTMENT QUIZ

■

Many of us in today's fast-paced, high-stress world find very little time to spend special evenings or weekends together, without children, away from work projects and briefcases, and just be alone with our mates. And because of our language barriers, many of us have not understood what our mates want or enjoy.

Make a commitment to invest in your marriage. Some of the wisest investments we will ever make are to sacrificially invest time, energy, planning, and effort into the growth, health, and success of our marriages. A workbook that we use in counseling people is called *Your Marriage Investment Portfolio.* Briefly, the workbook asks couples to record the investments they have made in the marriage from the time they met until the present. We believe you will find it helpful to do the same thing by answering the following questions.

A Love Investment Quiz

1. Did you receive premarital counseling?
2. Did your premarital counseling explore the differences in these areas: your families of origin, values, cultures, interests, hobbies, family histories, and how to relate to your in-laws?
3. Has either of you been married before?
4. Did you and your mate receive testing, such as personality profiles, career testing, language testing, temperament profiles, and the like, to discover compatibility, strengths and weaknesses, or interests?

5. What are the most valuable books you have read in your adult life that have affected you personally, spiritually, socially, and/or professionally?
6. Have you discussed these books with your mate?
7. What are the last five books you have read on *any* subject?
8. What books have you read that have helped you to learn how you can be a better mate?
9. Through reading, studying, and effort, have you worked out a more than satisfactory sexual relationship?
10. What books have you read that have taught sound biblical marriage principles?
11. What seminars, workshops, or retreats have you attended to help you learn more about your family or husband-wife relationship?
12. What newsletters do you subscribe to relating to the family, or family research newsletters and the like?
13. What Christian magazines do you subscribe to?
14. List the types of seminars and workshops you have attended or conducted within the last twelve months to improve your career, such as sales meetings, time management meetings, customer relationships, investment, or personal motivation.
15. List the business, professional, financial, and other newsletters and magazines you subscribe to.
16. Do you and your mate pray daily together, out loud?
17. Are you currently in a Bible study group? With or without your mate?
18. Do you and your mate attend church services together at least once a week?
19. Have you and your mate ever been in a couples' Sunday school class? Are you now in one?
20. Do you make a point to talk about your thoughts and feelings with your mate?
21. When you have a conflict, do you tend to get angry, leave or withdraw, or work through the conflict?

These are just a few of the questions you can ask yourself to determine if you are investing in your marriage.

The Point

> **MOST OF US SPEND LIFETIMES INVESTING IN OUR CAREERS, FINANCIAL FUTURES, PHYSICAL HEALTH, RECREATION, RETIREMENT FUNDS, AND SOCIAL ACTIVITIES. VERY LITTLE TIME, EFFORT, OR MONEY IS GENERALLY INVESTED IN THE MOST IMPORTANT ASSET WE HAVE HERE ON EARTH—OUR MARRIAGES AND FAMILIES.**

Marriage is God's first institution, not our careers. Marriage is our first ministry, not our communities, church, or the world. We will be judged by two things when we face God: how we treat our relationships with Him through Jesus Christ, and how we treat others, beginning with our mates and children.

With as little investment in our marriages as most of us have made (usually not even beginning much of an investment until there are major problems), it is a miracle that any of our marriages survive. Most people invest more time in getting driver's licenses than in improving their marriages, and both are life and death issues. It is very much like waiting until you are at retirement age before investing in your IRAs and 401(K) plans. If you are willing to invest time, effort, and a little money into moving from surviving to thriving, from hurting each other to helping and healing each other, from destroying your relationship to restoring your relationship, the compounded interest on your investment will truly be a hundredfold in this lifetime and the life to come. You will also be leaving an inheritance of marital blessings for your children and grandchildren.

Usually, when a couple come in for counseling, we ask them the investment questions. Even when their answers are mostly no, they still seem surprised that they are having problems. Marriage is like any other living entity. If it is not fed, watered, and cared for, it will die. Carefully pruned and tended marriages are beautiful, like English flower gardens. Untended marriages become choked by killing weeds and unwanted thorns.

Many times couples will say, "We can't afford counseling," or "We can't afford to go to that weekend seminar." Our question to you is, "Can you afford *not* to go?" If you do not make these important investments, the cost of divorce versus the cost of a good marriage can be destructive and devastating. Besides the lifelong, emotional trauma to all concerned, most persons suffer financial pressures and economic downturn following a divorce. Invest in your marriage—it is a bargain.

Investing in your marriage is investing in your health and joy, as well as those of your mate and children. And the best way to begin is to invest your time and effort in learning to communicate with your mate in his or her special behavioral language.

Now that you have begun to identify and use these languages, let's look at some specific ways that you can put these valuable communication tools to work for your marriage. The next four chapters will give you practical, you-can-do-it help. As you put these suggestions into action, consider this an addition to your Marriage Investment Portfolio.

> **FALLING IN LOVE IS EASY; GROWING IN LOVE MUST BE WORKED AT WITH DETERMINATION AS WELL AS IMAGINATION.**
> **—LESLEY BARFOOT**

**GOD SETS THE
SOLITARY IN
FAMILIES.**

■

PSALM 68:6

CHAPTER 12

Your Marriage Language Genogram

DRAWING A FAMILY PORTRAIT

■

Genograms are used in therapeutic settings to help us learn more about ourselves and our pasts. A language genogram is a format for drawing a type of family tree on which we record the languages of our family members over at least three generations. Through genograms, we look at parents, personalities, illnesses, addictions, broken relationships, disappointed expectations, hopes deferred, unrealized dreams, lasting commitments, healthy relationships, successes, and significant spiritual happenings. Genograms typically indicate women with a circle and men with a square.

We are looking at the genogram only for the purpose of language identification, realizing that as we discover more about our parents and children, we will also understand much more about ourselves: "You shall know the truth, and the truth shall make you free" (John 8:32).

Building Your Genogram

After you and your mate have completed the "Love Investment Quiz" in the previous chapter and have filled in your marriage language genograms in this chapter, you will discover your marriage language and family language.

Most couples discover that they have at least one behavioral language in common. However, if there is no shared language, look for a shared language category. If you and your mate have no language or category in common, that does not mean your marriage will not survive. It simply means you will probably have to develop your language communication awareness and skills to a greater degree. In other words, you have more of a challenge ahead of you, but your language difference may bring needed balance to your marriage, and a joyful marriage is definitely worth the effort.

Here is a reminder of the three communication-style categories and the behavioral languages that fall within each category:

Emotive	Cognitive	Kinetic
1. Responder	1. Strategist	1. Mover
2. Influencer	2. Contemplator	2. Doer
	3. Giver	

Before you complete your marriage language genogram, we would like to share ours (see fig. 12.1) with you to show how much valuable information you can gain by doing this exercise together. We have chosen to use the first letters of our primary and secondary languages to simplify completion of the genogram. The shaded blocks indicate the areas where our individual languages match. This is our easiest and most natural area of communication—our marriage language.

Fred's Languages   **Anna's Languages**

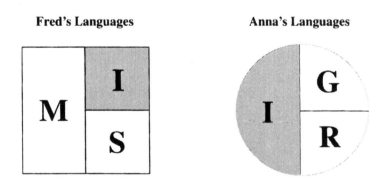

Fig. 12.1. Kendall Marriage Language: Influencer

Your marriage language is the communication style that you have in common with your mate. It is the most natural area of communication between you and your mate. It is probably effortless and easy for the two of you to relate in this way. Recognizing our marriage language as Influencer explained why we enjoy talking with each other. We easily communicate; relate; share feelings, thoughts, opinions, and ideas; and have fun together in this expressive language. We struggle in the other areas: Fred's Mover traits versus my (Anna's) Responder traits.

Fred's primary language is Mover, which is an action language. I do not have a single action language as one of my three major styles of communication. (It is in fourth place as Doer.) Naturally, my inactivity can be an area of frustration for Fred. Fred is always in motion, but I want to talk things through before I move into action. However, because Influencers like to play and have fun, my playful side can easily get hooked by Fred's exciting activity, and I will jump in for the fun or entertainment of it.

My secondary language is Giver (see fig. 12.2), which is a thinking language. This language makes me want to share materially, philanthropically, and generously with others, but since it is also a thinking language, that makes me stop and consider, reason, and look at my giving logically.

Fred's Languages   **Anna's Languages**

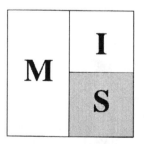   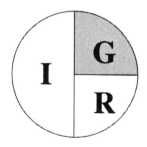

Fig. 12.2. First Marriage Language Category: Cognitive

Fred's Languages   **Anna's Languages**

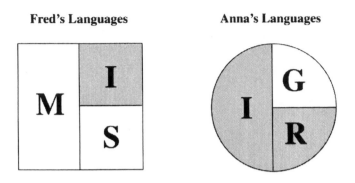

Fig. 12.3. Second Marriage Language Category: Emotive

Fred's third language is Strategist, which is also a thinking language. Although Fred does not share the giving and hospitality characteristics of the Giver, both the Giver and the Strategist are thinkers, which means that both Fred and I have a logical, reasoning side to our communication styles, giving us another area of marital compatibility.

My third language is Responder (see fig. 12.3), which is a feelings language. My primary language of Influencer is also feelings oriented. Fred's secondary language is Influencer, so he can speak the feelings languages. He can access his feelings, which is what the emotive languages do. That gives Fred and me still another area of marital compatibility.

So, in all, we have three areas of compatibility. We share the marriage language of Influencer, and we share two compatible language categories, which are emotive and cognitive.

Doing Your Genogram

Now it is your turn. In figure 12.4, fill in your three languages (one primary and two secondary) and your mate's three languages.

Look first for a match between your primary language and your mate's three languages. Using a highlighter pen, shade the two matching blocks. If there is no match, look for a match between your mate's primary language and your other two languages, and highlight

Husband's Languages   **Wife's Languages**

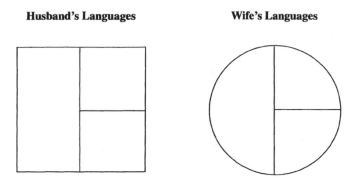

Fig. 12.4. Your Marriage Language: _____

the match. This match will be your marriage language. Use a different colored highlighter to shade a second set of matching languages. If there is no primary language match, any match at all becomes your marriage language. If, by chance, your primary languages have no match, but both secondary languages match, you will have a combined marriage language. Write the name(s) of the language(s) you have in common in the space provided on figure 12.4.

If you and your mate have no specific languages that match, look for matching categories (refer to the chart of categories and languages on page 188 in this chapter). Write that marriage category (or categories) in the space provided.

Recording Your Discoveries

Study your completed marriage language genogram carefully. Using a separate sheet of paper or a small notebook, write down any discoveries or observations about your ability to communicate with your mate. Answering some of these questions may help you come to some realizations and conclusions:

- What behavioral language do we share?
- What are the positive and negative characteristics of that shared language? (Refer to the appropriate language chapter for help.)

- How does that language communicate love to someone else?
- What past experiences in our marriage verify that we do, indeed, share this behavioral language?
- Thinking about how this language expresses love, what specific ways has my mate tried to say "I love you" in the past that I did not understand?
- What language category do we share?
- Is this category one of action, thought, or feeling? (Refer to the chart on page 188 at the beginning of this chapter.)
- What past experiences in our marriage verify that we share this approach to handling life, even though we may not have been aware of it until now?
- Considering the characteristics of our shared language(s), what specific things can we do to improve our love and communication? (For help on this one, refer to chapter 13: "Mates or Mind Readers?")

The Family Genogram

To gain further insight into your marriage and relationship, you will want to look at both families of origin. Your family of origin is the family that raised you. It might be your birth parents, foster parents, an older sister, or someone else who was your major caregiver as you were growing up. In this chapter we will simply refer to them as parents.

If your parents can be contacted, ask each of them to take the "Language Discovery Quiz" in chapter 2. If they cannot be contacted or are unwilling to take the quiz, take it for them, as best you can, and have your mate take the quiz for his or her parents, recognizing the results cannot be totally accurate but will likely be close enough to help.

You will be amazed at the valuable discoveries this exercise will help you make. You will begin to understand why you do or do not relate well to your parents and in-laws or why you may feel closer to one parent or in-law than the other. You will also gain great insight into how to improve your communication and relationships with your parents and in-laws by using the language information in this book.

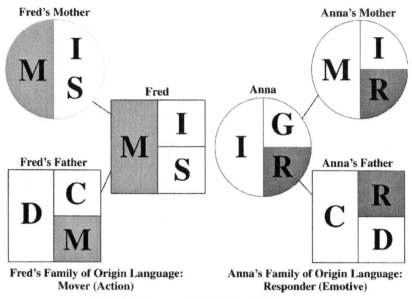

Fred's Family of Origin Language: Anna's Family of Origin Language:
Mover (Action)   Responder (Emotive)

Fig. 12.5. Anna and Fred's Family Genogram

We would like to share our family genogram (see fig. 12.5) with you before you complete your own.

I came into Fred's family not speaking either of the action languages of Mover or Doer. Needless to say, because I have no action language in my makeup, for several years Fred's parents and I did not understand each other or feel especially close to each other. When we visited his parents, everybody (except me) was very active. The whole family would be cleaning, painting, repairing, cooking, or doing some activity. All of them were doing something. Sometimes they were doing things together; sometimes they were doing things separately; but they were always doing something. Meanwhile, I stood around and did my natural thing—I talked to them while they worked.

Finally, I caught on to their language and made sure I was doing things, too, not just talking to them while they stayed busy. It was amazing how much our relationships improved after that. They no longer thought I was a lazy, different, or frivolous person, and I no longer saw them as possessed by a work demon.

As an Influencer, I could communicate with Fred's mom, whose secondary language was Influencer. We could always talk, and after I stumbled onto the action basis of their family language, we could talk and do things together at the same time, making everybody happy.

Our study of the behavioral languages has confirmed what other researchers have often said in the past: people often marry someone who reminds them of one or both of their parents. In other words, you may have some of the same characteristics as your mate's mother and/or father, and your mate may have some of the same characteristics as your mother and/or father. Let's look at the Kendall family genogram (see fig. 12.6) once again and make some observations.

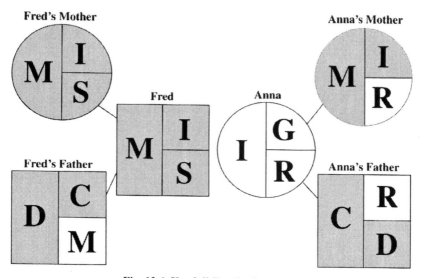

Fig. 12.6. Kendall Family Genogram

Notice, for example, how Fred's languages match my mother's languages. Fred has two languages in common with my mother, which probably explains why Fred is so close to her (and why they occasionally clash). This might also explain why I was so attracted to Fred; his communication style felt comfortable and familiar to me. He was much like my mother!

Perhaps you have heard a person say of his or her mate, "When we first met, it was as if I had known him (her) all my life." In a way that is true; he or she had known that person's behavioral style intimately all his or her life. This may even be where the phrase "love at first sight" comes from; there is an instant recognition (usually in the subconscious) of someone you have always loved (your parent) in a new acquaintance. We love this anonymous quote: "What's so remarkable about love at first sight? It's when people have been looking at each other for years that love becomes remarkable!"

You may also observe that Fred's three behavioral languages are *exactly* the same as his mother's languages, which is why Fred and his mother have always been very close to each other.

In contrast, I do not have a single language in common with Fred's father, which probably explains why although we loved each other, we struggled to understand each other through the years. Also note that Fred's father and mine have two matching languages, and as you might guess, my dad and I struggled to communicate, although not as much because my dad and I both have the Responder language in common.

Doing Your Family Genogram

Once again, it is now your turn to create your family genogram using the diagram provided in figure 12.7. Using the results of your parents' quizzes, fill in the diagram.

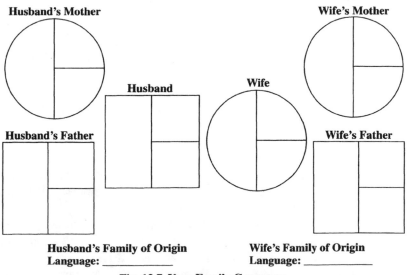

Fig. 12.7. Your Family Genogram

Recording Your Discoveries

After you have completed your family genogram, study it carefully. In the notebook you began earlier, or on a separate sheet of paper, record your observations and discoveries about the communication styles in both your and your mate's immediate families. Answering some of the following questions may help you focus on some significant points:

- What behavioral language(s) do I have in common with my parents? Does that help explain the kind of relationships we shared when I was a child, as well as now?
- What behavioral language(s) do I have in common with my mate's parents? Does that shed any light on the kind of relationships we have shared since I entered that family?
- What behavioral language(s) does my mate have in common with his or her parents? How does that explain the kind of relationships they have shared?
- What behavioral language(s) does my mate have in common with my parents? What insight does that give me about his or her relationships with my parents since we married?

Children's Genogram

Another important aspect of your marriage relationship involves your children, who have a dynamic impact on your household and the overall happiness of your marriage. For a more complete family picture, you will benefit from completing a genogram of you and your children.

This exercise will greatly help you to understand why there may be communication problems between you and your children. It will also help you know how to best communicate with your children effectively and how to help them develop their personal gifts and behavioral styles to their fullest potential.

From the children's genogram you will be able to determine your family language, like the family language you found when you completed the family of origin genogram (fig. 12.7).

Figure 12.8 is our Kendall family language genogram, which

involves Fred, our only child, Michael, and me. A study of the genogram revealed that all three of us do not share one behavioral language. So, we looked for common language categories and found several. We have a total of four cognitive or thinking languages, four emotive or feeling languages, and only one kinetic or action language. Since we have an equal number of cognitive and emotive languages, we concluded that our family communication style is a combination cognitive-emotive approach to handling life.

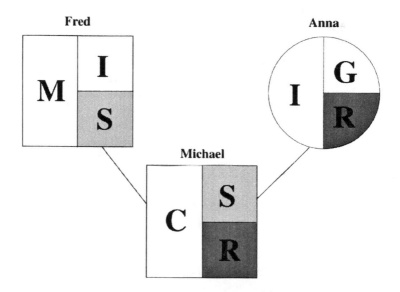

Fig. 12.8. Kendall Family Language Categories: Cognitive-Emotive

Here are some other interesting and helpful things we learned about our family:

- Fred and I are both Influencers who enjoy discussing ideas, thoughts, experiences, and feelings. We are quite happy chatting away, encouraging each other, lecturing at seminars together, and working together to motivate other people.
- Michael and I have our Responder language in common. We communicate very well on this plane because we are both compassionate, sensitive, and warm.

- Fred and Michael are both Strategists. They function together very well since they are both organized, visionary, and focused.
- Neither Fred nor I is a Contemplator, which is Michael's primary language in the cognitive category. However, both Fred and I have a cognitive language in which we are fluent. For us to relate as a family, I have to move into my Giver language, which is cognitive, and Fred has to move into his Strategist language, which is cognitive. Then we can relate to Michael through logic, reasoning, and thoughtful consideration. This is not easy for either Fred or me because both of us want to talk a lot, and Fred wants to be in constant motion. But understanding the languages has given us the insight to back off from our needs and to give Michael the three things his primary language needs: quality time together, time alone, and plenty of space. When we unselfishly give him what he needs, we honor his uniqueness, and our family grows together rather than apart.

Doing Your Children's Genogram

Before you can complete your children's genogram, you will need to ask each of your children to take the "Language Discovery Quiz" in chapter 2, if they are old enough and available. If they are not old enough or available, or if they are unwilling to take the quiz, you should try to take the test for each child as best you can, recognizing the results cannot be totally accurate but will likely be close enough to help.

With the results of the quiz, fill in the genogram in figure 12.9 for your oldest child. If you have more than one child, create a separate genogram for each on a separate sheet of paper or in the notebook you have begun.

Recording Your Discoveries

Now study the genogram of you and your child carefully, and record your observations and discoveries on a separate sheet of paper or in your notebook. Answering the following questions may help you identify some of the most important findings:

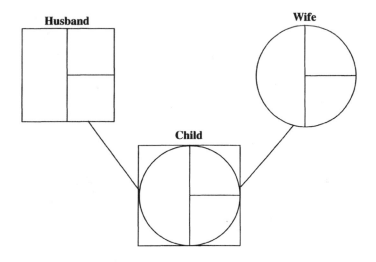

Fig. 12.9. Your Family Language or Category: _____

- Is there one behavioral language that all three of us share? If so, what are the characteristics of that language? (Refer to the chapter discussing that specific language to refresh your memory.)
- What language do I have in common with our child? How has that language been evident between us through the years?
- What language does our child have in common with my mate? How has that language been evident between them through the years?
- If there is no common language for the three of us, is there a language category that we all share? If so, what is it?
- What would each of us, as parents, need to change to better communicate with our child in his or her primary language?
- What can we as parents do, using the information in this book, to help our child develop his or her special gifts of communication to their fullest potential?

Sibling Rivalry

After you have completed the genogram for each child, take some time to study the languages of your children in relation to each other from the appropriate chapters of this book. What languages do they have in common? Where are their differences? Does their language difference help you understand why they may have trouble getting along or seem to constantly be in competition with each other? What other observations can you make about your children's communication with each other that affects the peace and joy of your family and, therefore, your marriage?

Bringing Down the Barriers

As a family, we have experienced the great thrill of tearing down the language barriers between us one brick at a time. No, we did not wake up one morning and find that the walls of Jericho had simply collapsed. Tearing down the walls between us is an ongoing, day-by-day effort. It is a commitment of love to continually work at learning each other's special communication styles and needs and then try to meet those needs. But, oh, the joy it brings!

May we challenge you to make a commitment of love to your mate and children to bring down the communication barriers by applying the information in this book on a daily basis? The rewards for your effort will be the greatest gift you can ever give yourself and your family—the beautiful gift of godly love and joy.

THE FAMILY BEGINS IN A COMMITMENT OF LOVE.
—JOSEPH AND LOIS BIRD

**BE KIND TO ONE
ANOTHER,
TENDERHEARTED,
FORGIVING ONE
ANOTHER,
EVEN AS GOD IN
CHRIST FORGAVE
YOU.**

■

EPHESIANS 4:32

CHAPTER 13

Mates or Mind Readers?

EXERCISES TO CREATE OPENNESS AND FORGIVENESS

■

At her golden wedding anniversary party, the wife told guests the secret of her happy marriage: "On my wedding day, I decided to make a list of ten of my husband's faults that, for the sake of our marriage, I would always overlook."

As the guests were leaving, a young woman (whose marriage had recently been in difficulty) asked the older woman what some of the faults were that she had seen fit to overlook.

The older woman said, "To tell you the truth, my dear, I never did get around to listing them. But whenever my husband did something that made me hopping mad, I would say to myself, 'Lucky for him that's one of the ten!' "

Speaking the Truth in Love

INTIMATE RELATIONSHIPS ARE BASED ON LOVE, OPENNESS, ACCEPTANCE, AND FORGIVENESS. A HEALTHY MARRIAGE EXHIBITS FREEDOM BETWEEN PARTNERS TO BE OPEN AND HONEST, AND IT THRIVES ON FREE-FLOWING FORGIVENESS.

Effective application of the love languages to your marriage will be greatly enhanced if openness and forgiveness exist first. This chapter will help you create them in your marriage.

> **PERHAPS NOTHING IS MORE IMPORTANT IN MARRIAGE THAN TRUTH AND HONESTY, BUT THESE ELEMENTS MUST BE EXPRESSED IN CONCERT WITH LOVE BECAUSE HONESTY WITHOUT LOVE IS AGGRESSION.**

Honesty without love can be deliberately painful and destructive.

The love God intended for marriage is pure and compassionate. We are to be highly concerned about our mates' feelings and needs. At the same time, we need to be free to voice our feelings to our mates, using wisdom and love in doing so. A vital ingredient in a healthy marriage is the partners' ability to edit their words so that they do not throw them at each other like daggers.

Our many years of counseling experience have revealed that most marriages tend to go to one extreme or the other. At one end of the spectrum, mates may not share feelings at all because they believe it is not important to do so, because they do not really know how to share them, or because they are afraid to share them. On the other end of the spectrum, mates share feelings in primarily negative, inappropriate, or destructive ways. Neither extreme is God's way of communicating through love.

God did not intend for us to deny or bury our feelings, nor did He intend for our feelings to control us. He gave us feelings to feel to indicate to us what we were experiencing. As individuals, we are much more than the sum total of our feelings, just as we are more than the total of our thoughts or our actions. We are first of all spiritual beings with souls, which involve our minds, wills, and emotions.

> **IT IS TRUE THAT WE *HAVE* EMOTIONS; IT IS NOT TRUE THAT WE *ARE* EMOTIONS.**

So, we can feel our feelings, acknowledge them, and share them, but we can also control our responses to them so that they do not inappropriately control us and our relationships.

When we deny our feelings, they are in control. Although they may be hidden from our awareness for the moment, they are still inside us churning around and will eventually cause physical and/or psychological problems. Medical science has proven through many research studies that suppressed feelings can lead to diseases, such as cancer, heart conditions, and arthritis, as well as disorders, such as depression, eating disorders, anxiety, and phobias, not to mention destroyed relationships.

We allow our feelings to be in control of us when our responses to feelings are out of control; thus, it appears that our feelings are controlling us and everyone around us. This may be through outbursts of anger, bouts of tears, emotional or physical withdrawal, instability, depression, phobias, or physical problems. If you and/or your mate have out-of-control feelings, help is available. God has appointed and equipped special people in His kingdom to help bring healing and balance back to you.

Forgiveness: Key to a Pure Heart

For marriages to grow and flourish in love, not only do we need the ability to be open and honest, but we also need to forgive each other on a continuing basis. We like what Mary (our coauthor) said about forgiveness in her book *Just Between Friends*:

> Forgiveness is not something we need, you and I, for I have accepted you as you are, and you me. You know that I am weak and make mistakes. I disappoint and hurt you, no doubt. But at the same instant you know it is without intention or malice. And I know the same of you. Because we have decided to be friends, we simply forgave each other once for all time—at the beginning.

When Jesus tells us to forgive someone seventy-seven times, He does not necessarily mean in a whole lifetime. If you take Him literally, when you reach number seventy-eight, can you stay angry? Sometimes it may mean to forgive a person seventy-seven times in one day or perhaps in one hour! Forgiving another person may be difficult because we mistakenly think that our forgiveness is also approval of that person's behavior. Forgiveness does not mean approval, but forgiveness prevents the hurt or rejection from moving into resentment, hostility, and bitterness.

FORGIVENESS KEEPS YOUR HEART SAFE.

Each of the seven behavioral languages handles forgiveness differently, but we all must realize that forgiveness is a necessary part of joyful living and loving in all areas of our lives, especially in our marriages.

TRUE LOVE CANNOT EXIST WITHOUT ITS BEST FRIEND, FORGIVENESS.

The Process of Forgiveness

Forgiveness must be an act of the will, a thoughtful decision. In our minds we must make decisions and then act on those decisions. Finally, we can allow our feelings to catch up with what we originally decided. We cannot approach forgiveness the other way around with our feelings first. Feelings can race up and down like a roller coaster running wild. They are undependable and illogical. In fact, our feelings most often block our path to forgiveness.

Because forgiveness is a godly concept created for our good, we must approach it first from a spiritual, biblical basis. A spiritual decision is more stable than logic. When we are having trouble making a logical decision to forgive someone, we can turn to God's Word to be reminded that forgiveness benefits us, not just the one being forgiven. This reminder will often kick our logic into gear and get us started down the right path. God's Word operates through our logic first. Then, the actions we choose to take in response to that logical decision are conducive to forgiveness, ones that propel us toward our goal. Feelings follow actions, and in time we begin to feel the healing and forgiveness as we act upon the decisions to forgive.

This process of forgiveness is important to remember as we deal with the three behavioral language categories: emotive, cognitive, and kinetic. None of these communication styles find forgiveness easy or natural. They must first be jump-started by the truth about forgiveness found in God's Word. Here's the bottom line:

WE DO NOT FORGIVE BECAUSE WE FEEL LIKE IT (EMOTIVE), BECAUSE IT IS LOGICAL (COGNITIVE), OR BECAUSE WE WANT TO REACH OUT AND GENTLY TOUCH THE ONE WHO HURT US (KINETIC). WE FORGIVE BECAUSE GOD'S WORD TEACHES US TO FORGIVE (SPIRITUAL), AND WE KNOW THAT GOD ONLY TELLS US TO DO WHAT IS GOOD FOR US BECAUSE "GOD IS LOVE."

Mates or Mind Readers?

"If you really loved me, you would know how I feel." Have you ever heard statements like this one? Or perhaps you have heard this: "You know I love you; I don't need to tell you all the time." Or this one: "I shouldn't have to tell you; you should know. . . ." But wait! Did we marry mates or mind readers?

The truth is, we cannot expect our mates to know our inner thoughts and feelings. No one knows them except us. And would we really *want* other people, even our mates, to be able to read our true thoughts and feelings? Probably not, at least not all the time.

The statements above are ludicrous.

NO MATTER HOW MUCH OUR MATES LOVE US, THEY CANNOT KNOW FOR SURE HOW WE FEEL UNLESS WE TELL THEM. AND EVEN IF OUR MATES BELIEVE THAT WE LOVE THEM, THEY STILL NEED TO HEAR US SAY SO.

Finally, why should our mates know how we feel or what we want without our telling them? If it applies to us, it should also apply to them. Can you read your mate's mind? Do you always know what he or she wants or feels? Even if you know your mate loves you, don't you like to be reassured and reaffirmed from time to time?

Regardless of the intensity of love and devotion, experience tells us that it is best for mates to say what they mean, mean what they say, and say how they feel to each other. Marriage partners should tell their desires and wants to each other. It is a serious disservice for mates to expect their partners to know everything about them just because they are married.

Commitment to Love

Speakers of the emotive languages—the Responder and the Influencer—most easily express feelings. Speakers of the other five languages have varying degrees of success and difficulty in expressing their inner feelings. Their ability may depend somewhat on their individual healing from past hurts, which could have caused them to shut down emotionally, or it may depend on their professional training and education in understanding the importance of sharing. Regardless of that, speakers of all seven languages have feelings, and all people need to be in relationships that offer the safety, security, and supportive atmospheres that are conducive to open, honest emotional liberty.

We challenge you to make a meaningful commitment to these two areas of your marriage: (1) providing a safe, secure, supportive relationship where your mate can trust feelings and thoughts with you, and (2) learning to share your feelings with as much honesty and openness as possible at this time. (Be aware of the difference between a thought, an opinion, and a feeling.)

I Feel Loved When . . .

Here is an exercise to help you start sharing your feelings. First, read through the different ways speakers of the seven behavioral languages might complete this sentence: "I feel loved when my mate says or does. . . ." Then, on a separate sheet of paper or in your notebook, complete the sentence for yourself and ask your mate to complete the sentence.

Influencer: "I feel loved when my husband calls me at work for no reason other than to say 'I love you.' I feel loved when he talks with me, and I feel loved when we do fun things together."

Responder: "I feel loved when my wife stops what she is doing as I walk in the door and greets me with a warm hug. And I feel loved when she sits beside me as we're watching television or when she really listens to my feelings and shares her own with me."

Strategist: "I feel loved when my husband shows me his acceptance through praise for the way I run my business and help him organize our life together. I also feel loved when we are in agreement about the goals for our lives."

Contemplator: "I feel loved when my wife plans quality time for us to be alone together without interruptions. I also feel loved by the quiet, peaceful atmosphere she creates in our home or when we have long discussions and I can share details on subjects I have researched."

Giver: "I feel loved when my husband gives me gifts, not only for special occasions, but also for no particular occasion. Those are the ones that say, 'While we were apart, I was thinking of you, and here is an expression of my love.' "

Mover: "I feel loved when my husband does things for me out of love and because he wants to do them. I also feel loved when he does things with me that are interesting or adventuresome. I feel loved when he accepts me for who I am."

Doer: "I feel loved when my wife does practical things for me. I also feel loved when she notices all that I do and tells me how much she appreciates what I do."

Now, how would you complete the sentence? Try to be as open and honest as you possibly can.

I Feel Frustrated When . . .

Let's try the same kind of exercise again, only this time, complete the sentence that begins, "I feel frustrated when my mate. . . ." Here are some examples of how speakers of the seven behavioral languages might complete this sentence.

Influencer: "I feel frustrated when my mate ignores me, leaves me out, or does not talk or listen to me. I feel frustrated when we do not have fun."

Responder: "I feel frustrated when my mate does not listen to my feelings or show affection to me."

Strategist: "I feel frustrated when my mate seems disorganized or out of control. I also feel frustrated when she does not give me the support I need to carry out our overall goals for our marriage."

Contemplator: "I feel frustrated when my mate does not allow me the time and space to be alone to think and work on my projects."

Giver: "I feel frustrated when my mate does not show excitement for the gifts I give him and when he does not participate in entertainment events and hospitality I show to others."

Mover: "I feel frustrated when my mate does not take action but just wants to sit around and talk, accomplishing nothing. I also get very frustrated when my mate's walk and talk do not match or when there are shades of gray rather than clear-cut, pure motives behind his actions."

Doer: "I feel frustrated when my mate does not do the practical things that need to be done. I also feel very frustrated when she does not appreciate all that I do."

Now, complete the sentence for yourself, and ask your mate to complete the sentence. Continue to be as open and honest as you can with each other.

More Feelings to Share

Continue exploring your feelings together by completing these sentences:

- "I feel angry when. . . ."
- "I feel happy when. . . ."
- "I feel sad when. . . ."
- "I feel excited when. . . ."
- "I feel guilty when. . . ."
- "I feel scared when. . . ."
- "I feel nervous when. . . ."
- "I feel sexually excited when. . . ."

After you and your mate have finished this exercise, set aside some specific time to talk about your answers with each other. We suggest that you truly *set aside* the time. Make an appointment with each other so that there is plenty of uninterrupted time in a warm, comfortable atmosphere. Pray together that neither of you will be defensive about the other's statements but that you will receive each other's feelings in a loving, nonthreatening manner.

REMEMBER, EACH OF YOU HAS A RIGHT TO YOUR FEELINGS; THEY ARE NEITHER RIGHT NOR WRONG; THEY JUST *ARE*.

We recommend that once a quarter or at least once a year you and your spouse set aside a weekend and check into a hotel with your only agenda being to do these exercises.

Mirroring

As you and your mate gently share your feelings with each other, practice mirroring each other's statements. Mirroring is an active-listening communication tool. It teaches the message receiver to listen more accurately and less defensively to the message sender. It will help the receiver to understand who the partner really is and to minimize misconceptions, false expectations, and projections. (Projection is a psychological defense mechanism where one person attributes his or her disowned and objectionable traits, attitudes, motives, feelings, and desires to the other person.)

Mirroring also helps the message sender to clarify thoughts and to communicate feelings and wishes more effectively. It helps the sender to feel more understood and valued.

WHEN SHOULD YOU MIRROR?

When your mate wants your attention and wants you to understand his or her feelings, thoughts, and beliefs, it is time to practice mirroring. Also, when you have an urge to reject, fight with, or avoid what your partner is telling you because you disagree with it or it makes you uncomfortable, it is time to practice mirroring.

HOW TO MIRROR

1. Let your mate finish a thought or statement (but stop him or her before you get overloaded with more information than you can assimilate). Say, "Just a minute, Honey. Let me be sure I have understood what you are saying."
2. Then restate or summarize in your own words what you heard and understood your mate to say (the meaning you derived from your mate's message). Then ask for confirmation.

"What I hear you saying is . . . ," or "What I think you are saying is that you do not want to spend Christmas with my family because you really do not like them. Is that right?"

3. Let your mate respond to what you mirrored back, listening for any new or different information from what you heard before. Your mate might say, "That is not quite what I meant. I do not want to spend Christmas with your family because I feel that *they* do not like *me*." (As you can see, this is a totally different message, and without the mirroring technique, the first partner would have misunderstood what the second partner was saying.)

4. To confirm the new message you have received, restate what you heard and understood. Say something like this: "Are you saying that until you feel liked or accepted by my family, you do not want to spend Christmas with them?"

5. Continue the steps above until your partner confirms that you have indeed heard and understood correctly. Then continue the conversation and process to reach an acceptable answer, solution, or compromise.

6. Proceed to share your views, feelings, and wishes. Take turns sharing and mirroring until you are confident that both are being understood. Mirroring brings understanding, which makes the mate who is sharing feel validated and accepted. He or she knows for sure that he or she has been correctly heard.

Remember to try to mirror your mate's statements in his or her behavioral languages rather than in your own, if possible. Do not embellish or interpret what you hear; just mirror it back as accurately as you can. For instance, a Mover husband might be tempted to add his interpretation of his wife's motive to what she said rather than just mirror her words.

Finally Speaking . . .

Creating openness and forgiveness in your marriage is vital to an ongoing healthy relationship. Having the freedom to express your innermost feelings and concerns without fear of rejection or retaliation is both exciting and joyful for you and your mate. This freedom allows you to be who you really are and to share your true self with the person you most want to know you intimately.

Not only will your verbal and emotional communication be vastly improved, but you will probably also find that both of you are able to express yourselves more freely in other areas of your relationship, such as sexual intimacy.

So, what are you waiting for? Now that you know how to relate to your mate openly, it is time to get started.

A HAPPY MARRIAGE IS THE UNION OF TWO GOOD FORGIVERS.

—*RUTH BELL GRAHAM*

WHATEVER YOU DO
IN WORD OR DEED,
DO ALL IN THE
NAME OF THE LORD
JESUS.

■

COLOSSIANS 3:17

CHAPTER 14

The Miraculous Words and Deeds of Love

WHAT TO SAY AND DO WHEN YOU DON'T KNOW WHAT TO SAY AND DO

■

Do you sometimes think that only miracles could rescue your marriage? Do you feel as if you and your mate are from different planets? Well, you are not alone. Our marriage and family were much less healthy until we put the languages of love into practice for us. And many other marriages have also been rescued from the divorce dumper with this new method of speaking of love.

This chapter will help you know specifically how to interact with your mate in his or her God-given style of communication or language of love. The first section will provide you with actual words, phrases, and sentences you can say in your mate's language to communicate your love in a way he or she can best understand. The second section will list specific actions you can take or things you can do for and with your mate to transmit the message "I love you."

If you are skeptical that simply changing a few words or deeds can make a significant difference in your marriage, we challenge you to try it before you reject it. The words and deeds of love worked for us; they have worked for other troubled couples; and they can work for you.

Miraculous Words of Love

When you want to speak lovingly and intimately with your mate, consider using some of the words, phrases, and sentences listed for his or her specific primary behavioral language in this chapter. These are, of course, a starting place. As you become more familiar with your mate's language, you will begin to develop more and more miraculous words and phrases that he or she loves to hear.

Emotive Languages: The Feelers

RESPONDER

Your Responder mate needs sensitive affection and understanding from you. He or she needs to hear words that describe feelings, such as these:

- "I feel. . . ."
- "Let's share. . . ."
- "I understand how you feel."
- "Sit here beside me and tell me about your day. . . ."
- "How do you feel about . . . ?"
- "Please tell me what's bothering you."
- "Let's talk about this so it doesn't become a disagreement."
- "Could we cuddle up, watch TV, and talk?"
- "I'm so sorry that my tone of voice hurt your feelings. I certainly didn't mean to sound that way."

INFLUENCER

Very similar in needs to a Responder, an Influencer mate needs more steps of action in your communication. He or she needs affirmation and encouragement from you, such as these words:

- "Let's talk about. . . ."
- "I understand how you feel about. . . ."
- "How do you feel about . . . ?"
- "What do you think about . . . ?"
- "What do you think we should do next?"
- "Tell me about your day."
- "Let me share with you about my day."

You will also want to use encouraging words like these:

- "That's great!"
- "You did a terrific job!"

- "I knew you could do it!"
- "You are wonderful!"
- "Tell me about your discussion of. . . ."
- "Let's do something fun together."
- "I love you."
- "I really love you."

Cognitive Languages: The Thinkers

STRATEGIST

A Strategist needs agreement and acceptance from you. Here are some words to use:

- "What do you think?"
- "Have you made plans for . . . ?"
- "I agree!"
- "I accept your decision about. . . ."
- "Let's set some goals for. . . ."
- "Would you tell me your overall plans for this situation?"
- "I appreciate the way you are always so prepared and have everything so well organized."
- "I know that leadership can be misunderstood, but I understand your mission [vision, purpose, goals, plans], and I think it's great!"
- "I love the way you make sure everything is done with excellence."
- "That is well thought out."
- "That's a great plan."

CONTEMPLATOR

To say "I love you" to a Contemplator, offer your uninterrupted attention and your sincere reassurance. Some of these sayings may help you convey how much you love and care:

- "What do you think about . . . ?"
- "Would you explain this to me?"
- "Let's close out all the interruptions and spend some quiet time together."
- "I understand what you mean about. . . ."

- "Could we research this and gather facts before we decide?"
- "What are you studying?"
- "You are the most important person to me."
- "Take your time; there's no hurry."
- "Could we please discuss this because I want to understand what you think."
- "Let's set an appointment to talk so that we have no misunderstandings."
- "Wow, you really are an authority."
- "I love the detailed way you explain. . . ."
- "You possess great depth and knowledge."

GIVER

Show your Giver appreciation and understanding with some of the following loving words and phrases:

- "What do you think?"
- "You are so thoughtful!"
- "I appreciate you so much."
- "Thank you for your generosity."
- "This is just what I needed!"
- "Your gift to me was an answer to prayer."
- "I am so grateful for you."
- "Your wise money management makes our home run smoothly."
- "I trust your decisions."
- "I know you listen to the Lord about our giving."
- "I am so proud of the way you entertain our guests."
- "You help make our home so warm and hospitable."

Kinetic Languages: The Actors

MOVER

A Mover mate needs approval, honesty, straight talk, and bottom-line information from you. Here are some ways to communicate your love to your Mover:

- "What can I do for you?"
- "Thank you for doing _____ for me."

- "I value your opinions."
- "This is what happened." (Then give it to him or her straight, no exaggeration.)
- "Let me share my reason or motive."
- "Tell me your goal or vision."
- "Let's go for it!"
- "Just do it!"
- "Let's do it now."
- "I'm ready at a moment's notice."
- "Let's do something exciting together."

DOER

Your Doer mate needs praise and approval from you for what he or she does. Try some of these sayings to create more love and closeness with your Doer:

- "What can I do for you?"
- "Thank you for doing _____ for me."
- "I appreciate all the many things you do."
- "I see all your hard work, and I really appreciate all your diligence."
- "I want you to know that all your efforts are noticed."
- "You always seem to observe what needs to be done when most other people don't even notice."
- "I appreciate how practical you are."
- "Nothing is ever left undone when you are here. Thanks."
- "You did a great job at _____ tonight."
- "The _____ looks great."
- "This is the best meal."
- "No one loads a dishwasher as well as you."

Miraculous Deeds of Love

In addition to what you *say* to your mate, what you *do* is important, even more important to speakers of some of the languages. This section will suggest some practical things to do with and for your mate in his or her behavioral language to express your love.

Emotive Languages: The Feelers

RESPONDER

Try some of these ideas with your Responder mate, and enjoy the love you receive in return:

- Give flowers, candy, and gifts.
- Send cards and letters for no particular reason.
- Give your Responder an abundance of touching, hugging, and holding in the atmosphere of togetherness. A Responder loves walking, shopping, having intimate dinners, caring for children, eating ice cream, going on picnics, and holding hands.
- Spend time together in worship, prayer, and fellowship.
- Show affectionate and sensitive sexual intimacy.
- Extend tolerance and patience toward skipped appointments or lateness in arriving.
- Understand when your mate seems "scattered" or disorganized.
- *Feel* with and for your mate. Set an atmosphere of trust where your Responder feels safe to share feelings, insecurities, or fears. You can do this during quiet walks, long talks, or cuddles by the fireplace.
- Offer lots of affection.
- Be patient, tolerant, and attentive.

INFLUENCER

An Influencer will love you for sharing yourself in some of the following ways:

- In conversations, share your thoughts, ideas, beliefs, and visions. Give responsive communication with many encouraging words and actions. They especially love these long talks over a cup of coffee or tea.
- Share your experiences, plans, feelings, and activities.
- Attend cultural events of music and art together.
- Laugh together. A shared sense of humor is important to an Influencer.
- Plan times of togetherness: walking, shopping, eating ice

cream, flying kites, going to amusement parks, and the like.

- Share worshiping, praying, studying the Bible, and fellowship.
- Send flowers, candy, cards, letters, and expressions of thoughtfulness often. A special occasion is not necessary.
- Listen carefully and pay attention when your mate talks. An Influencer needs your patience and tolerance, tenderness and nurturing.
- Participate in home decorating or creative projects.
- Make lots of phone calls. Your Influencer needs your contact and connectedness.
- Include lots and lots of friends in your activities!

Cognitive Languages: The Thinkers

STRATEGIST

Remembering that a Strategist is a thinker and planner, try some of these ideas to communicate your love:

- Share your thoughts, ideas, beliefs, vision, experiences, and plans. And listen to those of your mate.
- Study the Bible and fellowship together.
- Be serious with a serious-minded Strategist.
- Be sensitive to your Strategist's time and work pressures.
- Pay careful attention and listen actively.
- Accept differences.
- Express your appreciation for organization, hard work, and diligence.
- To say "I love you" to your Strategist, praise his or her God-given abilities.
- Honor his or her commitment to excellence.
- Be on time, and do not miss appointments. At least, if you must be late, call and explain.
- Keep your desk, bedroom, kitchen, office, and other areas organized, or at least visually uncluttered.
- Plan activities in advance, such as buying tickets for sporting and/or cultural events. Then carry out those activities as planned.

- Invite your mate to dinner in a lovely restaurant noted for excellent food and service.
- Plan travel with your Strategist carefully. Whether driving or flying, cross-country or internationally, plan it so that it all runs smoothly and is a quality event.
- Set goals together, and then actively pursue the goals. Plan vacations with your mate; plan family activities for the next year; plan budgets and other things.
- Plan, plan, plan with your Strategist, and then carry the plans out!

CONTEMPLATOR

This quiet, thinking person will understand your love through some of these deeds:

- Plan quiet meals and intimate dinners, sharing quality time with your Contemplator.
- Make something special for your Contemplator by hand, such as sewn work, artwork, and woodwork.
- Sit quietly with your Contemplator, not talking, just being together.
- Give your Contemplator mate plenty of alone time and personal space.
- Talk quietly, and share your thoughts, ideas, beliefs, vision, experiences, and plans.
- Listen carefully to your Contemplator explain something to you or teach you something he or she has learned.
- Provide companionship for such things as viewing movies with mutual friends, reading together, skiing, sharing music and art, and going to museums, libraries, antique shops, and other interesting places.
- Be serious, and talk about important topics and concepts.
- Be sensitive and gentle.
- Show your sincere appreciation for your Contemplator's abilities.
- Provide an accepting, low-conflict atmosphere for your Contemplator.
- Join your Contemplator mate in Bible study, small fellow-

ships, and biblical research to show you care about the same things he or she cares about.

- Research where you want to go on a trip, find out what there is to do, make sure you do not miss the important things to see and do, and enjoy it together.
- Search out quiet, intimate restaurants. Make a very special evening of it with just your mate, or take one or two close friends with you.
- Spend thoughtful, quality time together, and your Contemplator mate will know you love him or her deeply.

GIVER

To demonstrate your ongoing love to your Giver mate, speak in the language of giving. Here are some examples:

- Give gifts to your mate that reflect careful thought, attention, and appreciation for who he or she is. Give gifts for all occasions and no occasion at all.
- Share your inner thoughts, ideas, and plans.
- Receive the Giver's gifts with excitement, appreciation, and joy. Be a good receiver.
- Help your Giver mate entertain guests. Plan ways to show hospitality, such as dinner parties, cookouts, home fellowships, or small-group Bible studies. Be supportive of the need to entertain with grace and warmth.
- Be polite, gracious, and courteous. A Giver responds positively to these actions.
- Respect a Giver's money management abilities. Do not be a frivolous spender or too spontaneous in purchasing.
- Be open to discussions on giving to ministries and to people in need, as the Lord leads you and your Giver. Participate, support, and encourage his or her giving.
- Keep good records, such as budgets, household bills, and checkbooks.
- Plan and budget vacations; buy season tickets to activities (probably involving another couple as your guests); attend charity balls and benefits.
- To impress your Giver when you travel or eat out, use discount coupons, and buy the best quality for the best prices.

- Accompany your Giver to Bible studies, discussion groups, fellowships, prayer times, and worship.
- Give, give, give to show your love to a Giver.

Kinetic Languages: The Actors

MOVER

Being active and on the move is the way to communicate with a Mover. Here are some suggestions of things to do with and for your Mover mate to say "I love you":

- Get involved with what your Mover is doing: working, playing, shopping, or going somewhere.
- Plan exciting and fun activities to share, such as golf, tennis, snow skiing, jogging, backpacking, bicycling, board games, or other things.
- Be a companion to your Mover. Walk and talk; cook; go to ball games, movies, or antique malls. A Mover generally likes to share ideas, thoughts, and feelings while doing things together. So, keep your companionship active.
- *Do* things for a Mover. Cook favorite meals, organize closets, wash the car, mow the lawn, or clean the house. Being on the move is showing your love for a Mover.
- Take the time to give your Mover as much time and warmth as he or she needs.
- Pay careful attention and listen to your Mover.
- Be tender and nurturing.
- Stay in close contact and strongly connected to your Mover mate. Call him or her on the phone often just to say hello or "I love you" and to stay in touch as the Mover's plans change often.
- Travel together on long trips, short weekend jaunts, or a private adventure overnight in a hotel.
- Take your Mover to new, different, and out-of-the-ordinary restaurants.

DOER

Doing is the name of the game with your Doer mate, and here are some things you can do for yours:

- Share in activities: working, playing, shopping, cleaning, building, doing yard work, painting the house, organizing the drawers and cabinets, putting in new shelf paper, alphabetizing the books on the bookshelves, and on and on.
- Do things *for* your Doer. Cook favorite meals; clean out closets; wash the car. Anything you do for your Doer will be a message of love.
- Praise your Doer, and show special appreciation for all the things he or she does for you and for others.
- Accompany your Doer mate when boating; swimming; going to movies, the theater, flea markets, antique stores, lumber yards, or garden shops; having picnics; window-shopping; or doing anything interesting to them.
- Buy home improvement magazines, and plan projects to do with your mate all day on a Saturday or holiday, such as building a deck or window boxes. Plan and participate with your Doer in the ones that can be completed in a day or weekend or less.
- Go to practical restaurants, not the fancy or expensive ones.
- Do, do, do and be practical, practical with your Doer, and your love will be evident.

Express Your Love; Express Yourself

You can express your love in virtually any way you can express yourself. What is important is expressing it in a way that your beloved understands. It is not enough to think it to yourself; you must say it! Be fluent, proficient, and effective in the expression of your spouse's love language. And the return on your investment will be amazing.

LANGUAGE IS THE DRESS OF THOUGHT.
—SAMUEL JOHNSON

GOD IS LOVE, AND
HE WHO ABIDES IN
LOVE ABIDES IN
GOD, AND GOD
IN HIM.

■

1 JOHN 4:16

CHAPTER 15

Marriage-Building Weekends

ROMANTIC GETAWAYS BASED ON YOUR LANGUAGES

■

Making investments in your marriage is like putting money into securities. Most of the time you make small, regular deposits. Occasionally, though, you have a chance to make a larger, more substantial deposit, which greatly increases your overall investment portfolio.

> **MAKING INVESTMENTS IN YOUR MARRIAGE IS LIKE PUTTING MONEY INTO SECURITIES.**

Now that you have a working knowledge of your behavioral language and the language of your mate, it is time to make a substantial deposit into your Marriage Investment Portfolio. An excellent way to do that is to plan a special weekend with your mate. During this special time together, you can honor your mate by spending the entire weekend speaking your mate's behavioral language.

Why not spend one weekend that appeals to your mate's language, then spend another weekend in a way that appeals to your style of communication? By spending a weekend that really nurtures your mate and expresses your love in your mate's primary language, you will receive a wonderful return on your investment.

In this chapter we will suggest weekends that speakers of the seven behavioral languages would probably enjoy. Some weekends will be romantic; some will be active; some will be quiet. They are designed to particularly fit the desires and needs of speakers of each language.

Using our suggestions as a springboard, design a weekend that especially suits your mate. If you have a truly unique and successful weekend, we would like to know about it. Please write to us at the address in the back of this book and tell us about your special time together. Perhaps we can pass along your idea to other couples who speak the same language.

The Romantic Responder's Weekend

Romance! That's the name of the game for a Responder. Plan a weekend at a beautiful hotel or resort for just the two of you. Reserve the bridal suite, and arrange for all the romantic embellishments to go with it—flowers, candy, candlelit dinners. Spend the entire weekend showing your Responder mate lots of affection. Take him or her to a romantic movie, or rent one to watch together in your suite. During the movie, cuddle together.

Continue the weekend with a romantic dinner, perhaps at an Italian restaurant with strolling violinists, soft lights, and lots of talk about feelings and dreams. Do not talk about current issues or politics. Explore your feelings, relive happy memories, show your complete acceptance of your mate, and talk about happy plans for your future together.

Your Responder would also be happy with a picnic in the park or backyard, just as long as it has candlelight, soft music, hugs, kisses, and plenty of time to share feelings, hopes, and dreams. A Responder likes soft light and soft music in the bedroom, and your mate will reward your efforts to make the weekend romantic and emotionally stimulating. They also love to browse through old photo albums—remembering the wedding day or when the children were small.

The Interesting Influencer's Weekend

For your Influencer mate, plan an exciting weekend having fun together. Go to a big amusement park. Ride the rides; eat ice cream; laugh and talk together. Go to the city park and fly kites together, swing on the swings, or play Frisbee, just as long as there is plenty of time for talking and laughing together along the way.

In the evening go to a theater to see an upbeat performance, especially a musical. Then finish off the evening with a late dinner at a sidewalk café where you can watch the people going by before going to your hotel.

During the entire weekend, tell your Influencer in many different ways how much you love him or her. Use romantic, loving, affirming words. Share feelings and thoughts and dreams. And listen attentively as your spouse talks to you about feelings and hopes.

Be careful that your Influencer mate does not forget that this is a weekend just for the two of you. Otherwise, he or she may invite along a few friends because an Influencer loves to have people around.

The Successful Strategist's Weekend

Whatever kind of weekend you dream up to share with your Strategist mate, plan it well. Let your Strategist mate do the planning, but he or she may delegate it back to you. Schedule the special weekend well in advance so there is plenty of time to plan and make reservations. Leave nothing to chance. Your Strategist will love planning your evening so that each event is carefully scheduled. He or she may arrange for a romantic dinner at six o'clock, the theater at eight o'clock, and a quiet dessert back in your hotel room around eleven o'clock.

During your weekend together, talk about the goals, visions, and hopes for your marriage. Reestablish agreement with your Strategist mate on long-range life goals. Tell your mate how much you admire and appreciate his or her gift of keeping your life organized and running smoothly.

A Strategist may have an agenda of what to accomplish during the special weekend. Do not be surprised if he or she brings along a list of items to discuss or a special book like this one to read and study together between romantic moments.

Although this totally structured weekend may not be what you would choose for yourself, your Strategist will come home with a great sense of accomplishment and a strong feeling of closeness with you.

The Calm Contemplator's Weekend

Select a quiet, secluded, and romantic place to take your Contemplator mate for your special weekend together. Perhaps you can rent a small cabin in the mountains or a bungalow on the beach, or you can find a bed-and-breakfast in a small town where there are few distractions.

Make no specific plans other than just being together. Wander quietly through antique shops and bookstores; sit in the park and read; share your books with each other, whether you're reading history or romantic poetry. Ask your mate to talk about what he or she has been studying or learning recently. Walk through flower gardens; have quiet romantic dinners; enjoy breakfast in bed. Just be together, giving your Contemplator your undivided attention, with no hidden agenda and where no activity is as important as your mate.

The Generous Giver's Weekend

Your Giver mate will enjoy a well-researched and carefully planned weekend of romance. Because Givers are so aware of value, and since the thought behind the gift is as important as the gift itself, put a lot of thought into a weekend that meets your mate's special needs. Try to plan activities that you know your mate especially enjoys. A Giver will appreciate every aspect of the weekend being well thought out since he or she is not inclined to be spontaneous or just let things happen.

Many hotels offer special weekend rates that include dinner or breakfast in the cost. A Giver will appreciate the value of that. Try to use coupons or discount cards for restaurants and cultural events during the weekend, too. Unlike speakers of other languages who might consider your using coupons and discounts as a negative statement of your real love, a Giver will be impressed and appreciative.

Whether the weekend is in a fancy hotel or a quaint village inn, be sure your weekend includes a very special gift of love from you, beautifully wrapped in his or her favorite color and complete with a romantic card. Or you might consider giving your mate several small gifts, one every few hours during the weekend.

While you are alone together, pay special attention to being polite, considerate, and thoughtful. Use good manners at all times. Shower your Giver mate with appreciation for the gifts he or she gives to you and others—gifts of time, energy, money, and more. In a word, give to your Giver.

The Mighty Mover's Weekend

Since a Mover likes activity along with excitement, the challenge for you is to plan a weekend that will be romantic and include both. Choose a resort or hotel that has swimming pools, exercise facilities, tennis courts, horseback riding, a golf course, or other activities. Take advantage of as many of them during the weekend as possible with your mate. Then finish off the day with a romantic candlelit dinner.

Another option might be to take a bicycle (or motorcycle) ride out into the country and have a romantic picnic near a lake. If boating and water skiing can be included, all the better. Just remember that your Mover will be more open to communication and more romantic during or after the excitement and action needs are met. Whatever you do, keep moving!

The Diligent Doer's Weekend

An exciting weekend for you and your Doer is a mystery weekend. Because a Doer is very observant, tell your mate that this will be a surprise weekend, and that he or she will have to find and follow the clues to the surprise. Give the Doer plenty of notice about the weekend to get prepared. Then plan the mystery weekend carefully, leaving clues about where you are going, what you will be doing, and other important aspects of the weekend. Make the surprise at the end of the clues something wonderful that you know for certain your Doer will enjoy, such as a ride in a hot air balloon or tickets to a sporting event.

Another option with a Doer is a "to do" list weekend. Make a list of things you want to do together, and let your Doer mate check them off the list as you do them. The list should include favorite activities of your Doer, such as taking in five museums on Saturday, going to several hobby stores, or watching three old John Wayne movies.

On these special days, *do* everything you can for your Doer mate. Truly serve him or her in every little way you can, from driving the car to serving meals. Through it all, show your appreciation to your mate for all the wonderful things he or she does for you and others. Make him or her feel valued and prized by you.

Special Language Days

Prior to these special weekends, review your mate's primary behavioral language from the appropriate chapter in this book. Purpose in your heart to speak that language to the very best of your ability during the entire weekend.

A good exercise for you and your mate to do to keep your language skills polished for each other is to designate one day out of each month as a special language day. Perhaps the first day of the month is designated as "Responder Day," while the fifteenth day of each month is "Mover Day." On each particular day, do your best to speak that language all day long so that you can stay in good practice. Get into it, and have fun with the languages and your mate.

Your Seven-Room House

All of us have some measure of ability in each of the seven languages. All we need to do is exercise and develop those languages. We tend to get stuck in our own primary and secondary languages, which stunts our growth in the others.

You can view the seven languages like a seven-room house. You spend most of your time in the living room, the most comfortable room in the house for you. This is the room of your primary behavioral language, the room where you truly live.

Then you probably make regular trips into two other rooms. These are the rooms of your secondary languages. You do not spend as much time in these two rooms as in the living room, but they are familiar and comfortable.

Your house has four other rooms under the same roof, but you rarely go into them. These rooms also belong to you; they are part of your house; but you are not as comfortable in them. Figure 15.1 shows two house plans that illustrate Fred's and Anna's seven-room houses.

When you want to speak someone else's language, all you have to do is make an effort to move from your comfortable living room into that less used room of your house. Then you can do it. The more you go into that room, though, the more you will feel comfortable and "at home" there. If these rooms are where your mate and children live, should you not visit them more often so that you can build a warm and loving relationship with your family?

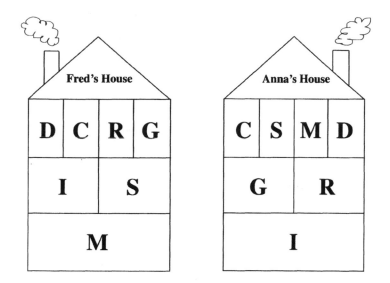

Fig. 15.1. House Plans

Making the Investment

> **THE TIME TO INVEST FOR THE FUTURE IS ALWAYS NOW. THE LONGER YOU WAIT TO INVEST, THE LESS RETURN YOU CAN EXPECT ON YOUR INVESTMENT. THE TIME TO INVEST IN YOUR MARRIAGE IS NOW; YOU CANNOT AFFORD TO WAIT UNTIL LATER; AND YOU CERTAINLY WANT THE GREATEST POSSIBLE RETURN.**

Why not begin planning that special marriage-building weekend right now?

> Love is enjoying the other person's
> enjoyment of you. If two people want to be
> enjoyed by one another, the only
> competition will be to outlove.
> —*Craig Massey*

LET'S EAT AND BE
MERRY! FOR THIS
MARRIAGE OF OURS
WAS DEAD AND IS
ALIVE AGAIN; IT
WAS LOST AND IS
FOUND. AND THEY
BEGAN TO BE
MERRY.

■

ADAPTED FROM LUKE 15:23–24

CHAPTER 16

Vive la Différence!

CELEBRATING GOD'S LOVE IN MANY LANGUAGES

■

Moving into the state of matrimony is like moving into a foreign country. It is strange to us in many ways. The culture is different; the people are different; the language is different. Oh, sure, we may have seen a few posters about it, and we have probably read a few pamphlets that describe its best points. Perhaps we have even gone to a travel agent and asked a few questions. It sounds like a nice enough place, but when we actually get there, the sights, the smells, and the sounds are all strange to us. People's hand motions, body language, and facial expressions are different. In reality, we have arrived in a world of foreigners and strangers.

Marriage is certainly like that. In addition to different family backgrounds, opposite ways of handling finances, varying ideas about disciplining children, and a myriad of other differences, there's often a huge communication barrier because you and your mate speak different behavioral languages. Even after twenty or thirty years of marriage, spouses do not always speak each other's languages fluently. In truth, the more we know about each other, the more we realize how little we really know.

Let's face it, folks:

MARRIAGES MAY BE MADE IN HEAVEN, BUT THEY HAVE TO BE WORKED OUT ON EARTH.

And living with another person is not easy, especially living with the opposite sex. That is because the sexes are *so* opposite in *so* many different ways!

Claire Cloninger, in her book *When the Glass Slipper Doesn't Fit and the Silver Spoon Is in Someone Else's Mouth*, described the miracle of marriage extremely well:

> I figure that the degree of difficulty in combining two lives ranks somewhere between rerouting a hurricane and finding a parking place in downtown Manhattan. I am of the opinion that only God Himself can make a marriage happen really well. And when He does it His way, it's one of His very best miracles. I mean, the Red Sea was good, but for my money this is better. What God can create out of . . . two surrendered lives is "infinitely more than we ever dare to ask or imagine."

The fact is,

> **HUSBANDS AND WIVES WILL NEVER BE THE SAME— NOT PHYSICALLY, EMOTIONALLY, INTELLECTUALLY, SEXUALLY, OR SPIRITUALLY. GOD DESIGNED US TO BE DIFFERENT, SO WHY ARE WE SURPRISED WHEN WE REALLY ARE?**

We are reminded of this premarital interview:

The preacher asked, "Do you take this man for better or worse?"

The bride answered, "He can't get any worse, and there is no hope of his getting any better, so I take him 'as is.' "

We have counseled couples who have been married for over fifty years, and they are still dealing with issues that were never resolved in the first five years of their marriages. They are recycling the same issues year after year. They never quite got past the "as is" stage. And communication (language) is at the root of the issue over 90 percent of the time. They simply do not understand each other's way of communicating.

Many couples come to us and say something like this: "If you can only change him or her so that he or she thinks as I do (or acts the way I do or feels about things the way I do), we will be happy, and everything will be wonderful." Wrong!

> **NO ONE ACTS, FEELS, THINKS, OR IS EXACTLY LIKE ANOTHER PERSON. GOD SPECIFICALLY CREATED UNIQUE INDIVIDUALS, NOT CLONES OR COOKIE-CUTTER PEOPLE.**

In a marriage there are many moments between the male and the female when the world does not look the same, and each wonders from what planet the other one originates. Both partners need to adjust their perspectives. If the marriage drifts into an adversary relationship, the marriage can be destroyed. But if we can learn to celebrate the differences, we realize that we are like two magnets whose opposite poles draw us together. The attraction *is* the differences, not the likenesses.

> **DIFFERENCES IN STYLES OF COMMUNICATION SHOULD BE ENJOYED AND, YES, EVEN CELEBRATED. THE MANY LANGUAGES OF LOVE THAT GOD CREATED WERE NOT MISTAKES. HE DID IT ON PURPOSE!**

He did it, perhaps, to put variety and interest in our lives. He gave us mysteries to solve about each other that can keep us entertained for a lifetime of love together. The differences are not our enemies; they are intended to be our friends.

Instead of being frustrated, we need to be fascinated with our mates' unique ways of expressing themselves and communicating their love to us. Instead of being irritated, we need to be interested. Instead of criticizing them, we need to encourage them to develop their special gifts and styles of loving that can complement our own. Instead of letting the differences pull us apart, we need to let them serve as magnets to pull us together forever.

When you have learned your mate's special behavioral language of love, you will create an epoxy bond between you that cannot be broken. You and your mate will be forever joined in heart, mind, soul, and spirit, and you will have learned how to celebrate the beautiful differences between you. We say, "Vive la différence!" May God bless you as you make speaking of love a priority in your marriage.

Apache Prayer of Benediction

Now you will feel no rain, for each of you will be
    shelter to the other.
Now you will feel no cold, for each of you will be
    warmth to the other.
Now there is no loneliness for you.
Now you are two persons, but there is only one life
    before you.
    Go now to your dwelling place,
to enter into the days of your togetherness,
    And may your days be good,
        and long together.

Addendum

■

Family Restoration Network, Inc.™ **(FRN)** is a non-profit corporation dedicated to strengthening the family, the local church, preventing divorce, minimizing the traumas of divorce, and helping create a healthy environment for children. Through FRN scripturally based workshops for churches and other non-profit organizations are presented.

Life Languages Institute, Inc.™ **(LLI)** is privileged to provide profiles, testing and workshops based on the Seven Behavioral Life Languages for businesses and governmental agencies. We are careful to always comply with EEOC regulations and are equally sensitive to the needs of employees and employers.

For information and catalog of workshops and resource materials, please contact us at the address below:

HELPING YOU SPEAK
THE LANGUAGES OF SUCCESS AND LOVE!©

LIFE LANGUAGES INSTITUTE, INC. ™   FAMILY RESTORATION NETWORK, INC.™

2711 Valley View Lane
Suite 103
Dallas, Texas 75234

Phone: (972) 406-1313
Fax: (972) 406-1299

YOUR SOURCE FOR THE KLLP!